THE NIGHT CLUB ERA

T0327041

THE
NIGHT CLUB ERA

By STANLEY WALKER

City Editor, New York Herald Tribune

With an Introduction by
ALVA JOHNSTON

THE JOHNS HOPKINS UNIVERSITY PRESS
BALTIMORE AND LONDON

Originally published in hardcover by Frederick A. Stokes Company,
New York, 1933
Johns Hopkins Paperbacks edition, 1999
9 8 7 6 5 4 3 2 1

The Johns Hopkins University Press
2715 North Charles Street
Baltimore, Maryland 21218-4363
www.press.jhu.edu

Library of Congress Cataloging-in-Publication Data

Walker, Stanley, b. 1898.
  The night club era / by Stanley Walker. — Johns Hopkins pbk. ed.
    p.   cm.
  Originally published : New York : Frederick A. Stokes Co., Stokes, 1933.
  Includes index.
  ISBN 0-8018-6291-4 (acid-free paper)
    1. New York (N.Y.)—Social life and customs—20th century.   2. Music-halls (Variety-
theaters, cabarets, etc.)—New York (State)—New York—History—20th century.
3. New York (N.Y.)—Biography.   4. Organized crime—New York (State)—New York—
History—20th century.   5. Prohibition—New York (State)—New York—History—20th
century.   I. Title.
F128.627.W26   1999
974.7'1042'0922—dc21   99-28135
                                                                         CIP

A catalog record for this book is available from the British Library.

INTRODUCTION

THIS is primarily a scientific book. It is a naturalist's investigation of the astonishing nocturnal fauna of New York—a monograph on the origin of some very strange species. Mr. Walker seeks by a wealth of anecdote and a cheerful ironic style to disguise the fact that he has written an authoritative work on metropolitan anthropology; but this study of modern gangsters, racketeers, hostesses, suckers, philosophical inn-keepers, killers, rats, parsons, columnists, cops, Federals and clip-joint proprietors belongs on the same shelf with Malinowski's "Crime and Custom in Savage Society," Cator's "Everyday Life Among the Head-Hunters," and Yerkes' "Treatise on the Chimpanzee."

The value of "The Night Club Era" for the general reader is, I believe, that it is the first organized and accurate story of the stirring changes in felonious and gay life in the New York of the past decade and a quarter. The millions of words which the average person has read on the subject usually have done nothing but make him more ignorant. The theme seems, as a rule, to produce in writers the same wheezing, epileptic style which a football classic produces in a radio announcer of the phony-emotion school. Mr.

Walker is different. His scholarship is infallible; he has a sympathetic understanding of his fabulous ca- naille; his presentation is lucid and unexaggerated; his wit strikes at you without warning from quiet, inno- cent sentences.

The value of the book to the scientist is its care- fully observed data of the response of the New York branch of the human family to reform stimuli. Bi- ologists have written volumes on the monstrosities and freaks which have been produced among fruit- flies and water-fleas by changes of temperature, diet, radiation and other environmental factors. The iri- descent Walker grotesques have had precisely the same origin. His gilded mugs, lawless altruists, massacre specialists and she-meteors of the night are all the products of prohibitions, curfews and other arbitrary interferences with the old environment. It was the last great effort of a narrow religion to regulate hu- man existence, and the indignant reactions of Broad- way biology are skilfully traced in this volume.

Stanley Walker is city editor of the *New York Herald Tribune*. Yet he is equipped to write this treatise. He is that rare article, a newspaper execu- tive who gets around a little and has first-hand knowl- edge of his town. He is a connoisseur of people, espe- cially fantastic ones, and seeks them out as the late J. P. Morgan sought rare old snuff-boxes. Fantastic people do not always wear well; Mr. Walker, however, is remarkable for a footwork like that of the late James J. Corbett in getting away from bores. He is a discriminating cop-fancier, and his passage on the New York police is a rare blend of realism with justice. One of his journalistic assets is a sixth sense; he either gets psychic tips or has a specialized imagination which furnishes him with intimations of the approach of unheralded events. He is practically a whippoorwill in his ability to forecast death, especially the death of an eminent citizen. In obedience to an intuition he called for the obituary of John R. Voorhis, the centenarian, and was revising it at the very minute when the venerable man passed on to his reward. He sent a reporter to get a birthday interview with the supposedly hale and hearty Simeon Ford, famous wit and after-dinner speaker, who died punctually on the reporter's arrival. It is probable that Mr. Walker has no more in him than mortal knowledge; his macabre instinct is probably a highly developed suspiciousness that something may happen, plus a passion for biography. His passion for the details of the lives of the great is manifested in this volume in the story of Owney Madden, a definite likeness of one of New York's most enigmatical figures. The vignettes of high-minded speakeasy proprietors and high-bosomed night-club dowagers are handsomely executed. Floods of white light are thrown, by means of these case histories, on the dark

and bloody age from which we are emerging. The
anguish of the Fundamentalist conscience over the
failure of New York to become godly is told with
pathos in the sketch of the late Dr. Straton, who was
the last of the grand old windbags of the New York
pulpit; who discovered that he was living in Sodom
and Gomorrah and gradually got to like both places;
who went in for faith healing and invented his own
system for eluding the Scythe, but at the early age of
54 forgot to duck.

Mr. Walker usually writes with contagious en-
thusiasm about his hyenas. The scaliest of them,
of course, have to be recognized as grisly little St.
Georges who rode forth as champions of civilization
against the dragon of Puritanism. Occasionally, the
writer betrays a prejudice against one of his gargoyles.
He takes sides against a certain gangster who, he says,
would shoot his own grandmother in the back and lay
bets on which way she would fall. Mr. Walker's sympathies are obviously with the dear old lady and it is
a fair inference from the text that he would not ac-
cept a bet as to the direction in which she would
topple.

The book has its national import, although dealing
chiefly with events that happened in New York.
New York is the chief test tube for social experiments
in America. Fresh religions, heresies, philosophies,
fads and trends start elsewhere, but their future is

commonly determined by their New York reception. The Federals recognized this. Their slogan was "Beat Broadway, and mop up the rest of the country at leisure," "Broadway" being like Wall Street or the Sargasso Sea, a loose term for a mass of phenomena rather than the name of a place. It was the violence of the Federal attack on New York which produced many of the violent deviations from normal humanity which are pictured in this album.

Nearly all the earlier books on gangs, racketeers, speakeasies and the good life have been marked by errors which a child could detect. "The Night Club Era" is distinguished by its conscientious accuracy. The only flaw that I was able to observe was an implication that Chauncey M. Depew stopped drinking champagne before he was eighty-six. It is on record, however, that at the age of ninety-three the Senator said that he still took champagne to cure colds, to which, he added archly, he was highly susceptible. But " 'The Night Club Era' should rate as a Broadway Koran. Other books on the subject are unnecessary if they agree with it, wrong if they differ from it, and in either case should be burned."

ALVA JOHNSTON.

CONTENTS

THE NIGHT CLUB ERA

THE NIGHT CLUB ERA

LAST NIGHT

THE Eighteenth Amendment went into effect on July 1, 1919, but the thing had no teeth in it. Many barrooms, facing the inevitable, closed, but many others remained open. A man could still get a drink. It was not until the night of January 16, 1920, that the Volstead Act, named for a droopy old gentleman from Minnesota, went into effect. After midnight there was prohibition, final and absolute. It was illegal to sell or transport any beverage containing more than one-half of one per cent of alcohol. Eleven days before, nine aged thinkers on the bench of the Supreme Court of the United States had voted, five to four, that there was nothing in the prohibition law which went contrary to the hallowed rights of the states.

New York, home of the great barrooms, the gorgeous hotels, the gaudiest cabarets in all history, had seen it coming, but even now it didn't seem quite real. Old-timers were puzzled, incredulous, and they asked each other: "Will they really try to enforce that

damn fool law?" An experienced bartender named
Bleeck buttonholed Representative Christopher D.
Sullivan, of the East Side Sullivans, and asked:
"Christy, are they really going to enforce it?" And
Christy replied: "Yes, I think so. There won't be any
more liquor." In later years they laughed at the
memory of this curiously naïve conversation.

As midnight approached the weather became terribly cold. A bitterly chill wind swept around the
corners. Derelicts huddled in hallways, and tried to
sleep under piles of old newspapers. The blanketed
horses arched their backs and hobbled along on the
icy pavements. Snowplows crunched through the
streets. The little gallery which always watched the
presses run under the sidewalk at the doge's palace
which James Gordon Bennett had erected for his
Herald in Herald Square had thinned to a mere handful. It was too cold to watch the dying writhings
of that old paper. After midnight the temperature
in the city went down to six degrees above zero; upstate, at a place called Big Moose, it was forty-seven
below.

This night of the dismal Sixteenth was one of incredulous sadness, of silly high jinks; there was gaiety,
with overtones of mockery. New York, along with
Chicago and New Orleans and St. Louis and San
Francisco and all the other centers of high-toned
drinking, met the grim midnight with farewell par-

ties for John Barleycorn. A few mourners hung around some of the old bars—some of which already had been turned into speakeasies. The greatest of these bars were to gather cobwebs for many a long and bloody year.

In some of the hotels there were elaborate wakes. Those which had not already turned their bars into soft drink counters, or leased them out as stores, or boarded them up against the coming of a miracle, left them open and bare for a time, inviting bankruptcy. Curiously, most people on that long-ago night seemed to think that the country was really going dry. The fight had been too long, too determined, and no amendment could ever be repealed. In a few clubs, cheery places which would be rookeries without booze, little groups of seasoned, embittered drinkers said that it wasn't true. It couldn't last. Egad, sir, these bluenoses can't tell us not to drink! Repeal would come. "Maybe not in your lifetime or mine, my boy, but it will come."

It was victory for William Jennings Bryan, who was to die in Tennessee years later after a heavy meal; for Mrs. Ella A. Boole of the W.C.T.U., who was to live to see legal liquor come back, and for William H. Anderson, superintendent of the New York State Anti-Saloon League. Mr. Anderson, magnanimous in his triumph, told the drinker: "Be a good sport about it. No more falling off the water wagon.

Uncle Sam will help you keep your pledge." Millions groaned, and gave him that derisive, horrific, shockingly vulgar retort which later came to be known as the Bronx cheer. These same millions, a few years later, chortled when Ferdinand Pecora, as Assistant District Attorney of New York County, sent Mr. Anderson to Sing Sing for third degree forgery—a pretty feeble degree of forgery, but enough to send him to Sing Sing, anyhow.

On this last night, down on New York's lower East Side, Louis Zeltner, a character known as "Wireless Louie," at one time an Alderman and at other times a tipster on the strange goings-on in New York City, was master of ceremonies at a wine-bibbing party at Max's Little Hungary. Already Zeltner was a friend of Izzy Einstein and Moe Smith, who were to become the most widely publicized of all prohibition agents; they were friends, yes, but Zeltner, who made money by tipping newspapers to the news of their more amusing raids, always regarded their snooping as somehow anti-social.

Uptown, at Maxim's, the waiters were dressed as pallbearers. At Reisenweber's there was a funeral ball, and Louis Fischer, boss of the place, was one of the saddest men in town. He was doomed to be sad for a long time, but after thirteen lean and lonely years he was to get a job handing out licenses for 3.2% beer.

At the Majestic, Dan Healy, a bottle sticking from his hip pocket, impersonated Rollin Kirby's cartoon figure of Prohibition—the gaunt, cruel-lipped chap with the funereal get-up, the high hat and the suspiciously boozy nose. Mr. Healy couldn't know that night that Kirby's symbol would be the wraith which, along with Dr. Nicholas Murray Butler, Alfred E. Smith, Mrs. Charles H. Sabin and a few others, was to turn the country against the dry law.

The Café de Paris, formerly Rector's, gave a Cinderella ball; Nellie King and her daughter, Edna Goodrich, who married Nat Goodwin, the fanatically uxorious actor, were there.

Corse Payton, who called himself the world's best bad actor, was at Jack Dunston's restaurant in Sixth Avenue (the fabulous "Jack's" of the flying wedge of Irish waiters who could heave a college boy halfway across the avenue if so minded) early in the evening, but soon tiring of the merciless jests directed at him by Wilson Mizner, he went up to Reisenweber's.

Nora Bayes, Al Fields, Bessie McCoy Davis (the Yama-Yama girl who was the widow of Richard Harding Davis) and Lillian Russell's daughter Dorothy were at a party up in Larchmont.

Joel Rinaldo, the saturnine, sandy-haired proprietor of Joel's restaurant in Forty-first Street just west of Seventh Avenue, watched his customers eat his overrated chili con carne. He was pondering a scheme for eluding the enforcers of prohibition by serving his drinks in teacups. Joel, author of that amazing, goofy and erudite work which he called "The Polygeneric Theory of Life," remained in business for more than four years after that night. Then he retired to Brooklyn, there to drink brandy and to ponder the more inscrutable aspects of creation.

DeWolf Hopper, much-married actor and declaimer of "Casey at the Bat," walked out of the clubhouse of the Lambs on Forty-fourth Street and told a friend (it was an old jest even then, Heaven knows) that when he died he was not to be buried, but turned over to a competent taxidermist, stuffed and placed among the statues in front of Amelia Bingham's house on Riverside Drive.

Randolph Marshall, handsome wisecracker in the days before they called them wisecrackers, coiner of inverted witticisms which are remembered by gaffers from Alberta to Sandy Hook, was in Philadelphia that night, drinking Scotch from a bottle. It was Marshall, the best researches show, who first suggested that Macy's window be used for something besides the display of merchandise. And the time he fixed for the startling scene was not high noon, as is often erroneously supposed, but three o'clock in the afternoon, when the shopping rush was at its greatest.

On the night of the Sixteenth, up in the Berkshire School at Sheffield, Massachusetts, a tall, grave-faced boy named Lucius Morris Beebe, already a Tory and a Republican by upbringing and instinct, was developing a fondness for strange phrases, for Horace, and for iridescent images. Nine years from that night he was in New York, starting the career which was to make him the outstanding dude among the journalists—one of the town's figures, whose top-hat could be seen at all opening nights, who could discourse for hours on fine wines, who worshiped the memory of the great Evander Berry Wall of the boulevards, who chartered a sleigh to ride through Central Park at the first big snowfall, and who one afternoon used a shotgun to bring down some balloons which had escaped in the Metropolitan Opera House. Always a baiter of peasants, he cursed the low, inbred hillbillies who, he contended, were responsible for the prohibition law.

On this same night Bat Masterson, the able gunfighter of Dodge City days, who even then seemed like a moth-eaten character from some long-forgotten drama, toiled over the halting prose which went into his column on prizefighting at the *Morning Telegraph,* then housed in the old car-barns at Eighth Avenue and Fiftieth Street. Just before midnight the creaky Bat walked down to Shanley's, took a table in a corner and sat there brooding over a steak sandwich and a cup of tea. The Bat, who in his day could have whipped any one of the mobs which were to

infest Broadway, died before New York had blos-
somed into something infinitely more dangerous and
sinister than Dodge City or Tombstone ever were.

Jake Wolff, who once had been proprietor of the
old Casino Bar, where John L. Sullivan, James J.
Corbett and Maurice Barrymore had once had drinks,
was prepared to pass the rest of his life without wor-
rying over either the selling or the drinking of liquor.
A man of incomparable dignity, who looked like
something out of Dickens, or an old English tavern
print come to life, he passed the long years sitting or
standing in hotel lobbies. For ten years after prohibition he haunted the Astor lobby, and then he went
to the Taft, where, he said, the sitting was more to
his liking, although there had been some mighty fine
sitting down at the Astor.

Charles E. Chapin, the hard-boiled editor with the
cold, light-blue eyes, was in Sing Sing for the murder
of his wife. He was getting out a paper there, a sort
of house organ for the inmates, and was beginning
to take an interest in gardening. A year or so later
he began his famous love-letters to foolish women on
the outside—those missives which somehow read like
the love-calls of a senile nightingale. Also in Sing
Sing was Owen Madden, who cared more for pigeons
than Chapin did for his roses. Chapin, who once had
loved fine wines, was to stay in prison and die; Mad-

den was to come out in three years for a nine-year period as the master of the New York rackets.

Enrico Caruso, who had married Dorothy Park Benjamin, had become the father of little Gloria and was living at the Knickerbocker, where they had the bar with Maxfield Parrish's painting of Old King Cole above it—the painting which now is in the Racquet and Tennis Club. Soon Caruso was to move to the Vanderbilt, where he barely lived through a siege of pleurisy, during which statesmen and Italian laborers crowded into the lobby to inquire about his condition. Then he got better and went to Italy to die, and when word came that he was gone women walked down Broadway weeping. To him, who was fond of spaghetti and wine and horseplay and heavy jests, the prohibition law was sheer insanity.

Chauncey M. Depew, doubtful of the wisdom of prohibition, had just accepted an invitation to make a speech at a lunch of the Pilgrims at the Plaza. No need to do much work on it; these things came easily to him. Nearing eighty-six, he said he felt fine, but the cords of eloquence had begun to quaver a bit. Long ago he had given up the pleasures of the grape.

William J. Fallon walked up Broadway, sniffed the air and found it good. What did it matter if it was cold? And what did prohibition matter? There would always be booze, one way or another. This remarkably handsome and talented young lawyer was a leader of that aggregation of sharp lads who were called the Broadway and Forty-second Street Bar Association. He had come down from Westchester County, where he had made an almost perfect record as a prosecutor in murder cases, and was settling down as a lawyer for the defense. Already Fallon, on prohibition night, was starting on the dizzy, boozy highway littered with bottles and women. An engaging and endlessly profligate man, who cut his own hair and didn't care whether his shoes ever were shined, he was to die such a few years later in a little uptown hotel—broke, wrecked in health, in virtual disgrace, although he had cleared himself of every charge ever brought against him.

On the night of the Sixteenth a pasty-faced man named Joseph Bowne Elwell, turfman, gambler and bridge whist expert, lover of many beautiful women, went early to his home in the West Seventies and pulled on one of his many silk dressing gowns. He was at the top of his career as an adviser to New York society on the fine points of gaming. Although he was somehow unwholesome, physically undistinguished, and wore a toupee, all women seemed attracted to him. Prohibition meant little to him, but sex and money did. Early one morning in June, 1920, he was found murdered in his home. No one ever was brought to book for the killing.

Arnold Rothstein, the walking bank, the pawn-

broker of the underworld, the furtive and unhealthy
man who sidled along the doorways, was sitting in
on a card game the night prohibition struck New
York. Not yet had he been openly accused of fixing
the World Series of 1919, nor would he be until the
next October, although a few men wondered even
then why he had bet such enormous sums that Cin-
cinnati would win the first game if he didn't "know
something." Years later Rothstein's passing was to
be another great murder mystery: who had shot him
just before he was found dying at the side entrance
of the Park Central Hotel? He died in Polyclinic
Hospital while Herbert Hoover was beating Al Smith
for President of the United States.

Alphonse Capone, a Brooklyn boy who had already
achieved a slight but not necessarily promising reputation with the old Five Points Gang, or what was
left of it, had been discharged from the Army in
1919, and his vision was so limited, his reasoning so
immature, that the coming of prohibition meant next
to nothing to him. It would not be long, however,
before he would listen to Johnny Torrio and go to
Chicago, to start his flaming career in one of Torrio's
brothels.

Dr. Charles H. Parkhurst, the old clergyman whose
denunciations of vice and graft, and official complacency, led to the fruitful Lexow investigation before the turn of the century, said he wasn't so sure

that prohibition would work, human appetites being what they were, but he was the enemy of booze anyhow. At seventy-eight, he stroked his whiskers, said there was a lot of good in the world in spite of Tammany, admitted that when he was an investigator he had downed a lot of liquor and carried it like a man, and announced that what the world needed was leadership, with General Wood for President. He died in September, 1933, after falling off a roof while walking in his sleep.

Evelyn Nesbit Thaw, over whom Harry K. Thaw killed Stanford White on the roof of old Madison Square Garden, was being sued for divorce by Jack Clifford (Virgil James Montagni). This divorce was granted, set aside, and then kicked about for more than thirteen years, so that the eager public reached the point where it didn't care whether she was divorced or not. At prohibition, whatever glamour Miss Nesbit once had was gone. She was a tired, nervous little woman trying to make a go of a tearoom just off Broadway in the West Fifties. She passed most of the prohibition era in cabarets in Atlantic City, where Shriners, Elks, Rotarians and hardware merchants, there for conventions, came to gape and nudge each other as they wondered what she had looked like that night of "Mlle. Champagne" on the roof of the old Garden.

On prohibition night a shambling, repellent figure

of a man, with a face like that of a cunning, malevolent gorilla, buttoned his coat tightly about him and walked east from the Blue Bird Café on Fourteenth street. He was Monk Eastman, gangster and war hero, whose body carried the scars and slugs from the small, relatively unimportant wars in which he had engaged before he enlisted for his country. It was not long after this night that his rackets, vaguely connected with illicit alcohol, got him into trouble, and one morning he was found, shot to death, lying in the Fourteenth Street gutter near where he had been accustomed to steer his nightly course.

Frank A. Munsey, the lonely publisher who never had learned to play, and who fumbled in his strangely wistful fashion to get some pleasure out of life, had just bought the New York *Herald* and on the night of the Sixteenth was sitting in a conference with his advisers in his apartment at the Ritz-Carlton trying to decide what to do with it. Two weeks later he announced that he was going to merge it with the morning *Sun,* retaining the best features of each.

There was something unusual and faintly unnatural in the air. A few educators had begun to worry about the younger generation. On the surface virtue was triumphant. The New York police had chased the streetwalkers indoors; prohibition finally had been riveted in the body of the law; woman suffrage was sure to have a marvelously regenerative effect upon the body politic; prices were high and most people were prosperous, spending enormous sums for automobiles and jewelry. And yet something was wrong.

It was (the phrase was a long time in the coining) the post-war moral let-down. People had been pulled away from their old moorings. Tradition had been uprooted and all that sort of thing. Did a young man kill another one over a truckload of booze? Ah, well, that would pass, and we must remember that the boys have just been through a terrible war, where they learned to use guns and shoot people. One must not judge the law by such unfortunate instances.

Then skirts got shorter, petting in automobiles was reported from some of the outlying precincts, some of the youngsters were reported to be drinking bootleg booze. The police and surety companies were worried about the increase in payroll robberies. These were the premonitory rumblings of the great crusade to make people good, the first head-shakings at the carryings-on of the gin-crazed flapper and her boy friends. There was a moral let-down, all right, and it was heard round the world.

The politicians and their advance agents were making curious noises. Only a few stubborn old curmudgeons, who were openly accused of being either hopeless drunkards and lechers or in the pay of the distilleries, insisted that there should be kept alive in both political parties a strong sentiment against prohibition. For the most part the politicians, fearful of the forces which had made prohibition the law, preferred to forget the issue and look for other game.

Everyone knew that the next President would be a Republican. On mild days President Wilson, over whose veto Congress had passed prohibition, was adjudged well enough to be wheeled about the White House grounds. He was a broken man, his face aged and twisted by pain. The end, obviously, was not far off. Who would get the Republican nomination?

General Leonard Wood, whose backers always insisted that he was a well man, although he finally died of the same brain ailment which his intimates knew he had suffered from before, was almost frantically eager for the nomination. Dr. Nicholas Murray Butler was spoken of highly, and not alone by Dr. Butler. Up in Massachusetts Calvin Coolidge, the Governor, had just delivered an electrifying message to the Legislature in which he came out flat-footedly, foursquare and uncompromisingly with the declaration that he favored obedience to law. Some of his friends were saying that he was excellent Presidential timber; they were, as it turned out, extremely modest, for their candidate also was to become the First American Philosopher. Herbert Hoover, back from relief work in Europe, was conferring with his loyal group of admirers in New York. Already the Hoover propaganda machine was beginning to work.

Somebody said that he was a Progressive Republican, but at this time no one seemed to know for a certainty. There was some talk that Franklin D. Roosevelt, Assistant Secretary of the Navy, who came of a good family in Dutchess County, New York, might run for United States Senator. Instead, he was to run that year for Vice-President on the Democratic ticket with James M. Cox of Ohio. Only one man thought Roosevelt might some day be President, and that was his eloquent little aide, the gnome-like Louis McHenry Howe, who in later years, because Governor Ruby Laffoon of Kentucky dubbed him so, was to be known jestingly as "Col." Howe.

Over in New Jersey Governor Edward I. Edwards, whose avowed dream was to make New Jersey as wet as the Atlantic Ocean, was hopeful that he could nullify prohibition by a state law legalizing the sale of light wines and beer. His hope of doing this legally was an utter failure, but New Jersey, if anything, went right on being wetter than the Atlantic Ocean. In the backwoods the peasants guzzled their Jersey lightning, a dreadful dose; in the hills and orchard country they had their applejack; the state's drugstores and speakeasies spouted rye, Scotch and gin, and many of the largest breweries continued without pause to turn out potable beer. Poor Edwards, who later served honorably in the United States Senate, finally killed himself because of an incurable illness, long before there appeared to be any immediate hope for repeal of the Eighteenth Amendment.

Just before the night of the Sixteenth 30,000 barrels of excellent whisky, valued by some experts at $70,000,000, was shipped abroad. This precious stuff had been held in Kentucky and Pennsylvania for export, and the owners had to get it out of the country before prohibition, final and irrevocable, went into effect.

In this fabulous period two visiting celebrities were being fawned upon. They were in the great postwar rush of lecturers. The American audiences, their appetites whetted by listening to foreign propagandists during the war, were eager to pay money to listen to any foreigner, however hoary his ideas at bottom, who had a Message. Lee Keedick brought over Sir Oliver Lodge, and James B. Pond had in tow Maurice Maeterlinck. Pond and Maeterlinck were squabbling over a contract. The dreamy Belgian had just lived through the celebrated fiasco at Carnegie Hall, where his lecture, delivered in a peculiar phonetic English which he had worked out for himself, had proved to be just so much gibberish to the audience. Then, when the great man switched in mid-lecture to French, most of the audience were just as much in the dark as ever. It was all pretty messy. Sir Oliver, who could speak English, and who stuck to his amiable Poltergeister from the other world, did much better.

This night, the old Sixteenth, was the twilight of human liberty. A. Mitchell Palmer was Attorney General of the United States. The right-thinkers were in the saddle. Emma Goldman and her little crew had been deported on the *Buford*, but that was not the end. In thirty-five American cities there was a round-up of radicals of all shades; in New York alone more than 650 men and women were taken to the old Department of Justice headquarters at 21 Park Row, and more subversive thinkers were being sought on warrants.

Agents dragged the reds and the pinks from their hiding-places all over town, particularly from the neighborhood of Union Square, where, years later, Soviet orators, admittedly in the pay of Moscow and frankly demanding that the revolution come to the United States, were accorded every courtesy and protection by the police. Not much came of all this excitement, but it had the town in a seething frenzy while it lasted. Some people even went so far as to advocate the hanging of all Socialists, not to mention Communists.

Indeed, the five Socialists who had been elected to the New York State Assembly were in the midst of a bitter and amusing fight. The Assembly had barred them on the indictment that they were against the

government of the United States and of the state
of New York. Even in this dark period, however,
there were a few voices who spoke up to ask, what
the hell? Alfred E. Smith, then Governor, took the
part of the Socialists, even at that early date justify-
ing the characterization that "Al is really a very
stupid man; all he can see is the point." Others who
swung into action for the ousted five were Charles
Evans Hughes, Morgan J. O'Brien, Joseph M. Pros-
kauer, Louis Marshall, Ogden L. Mills and John G.
Milburn. So great was the hysteria that few persons
knew the difference between a Communist and a
Socialist. However, the fight for the Socialist As-
semblymen made it safe forever after for a Socialist
to run for any office; indeed, in the years that followed, the Socialist Norman Thomas became one of
the town's most beloved public figures, and Heywood
Broun was allowed the freedom of the city, to ful-
minate or to incite.

It was terrific while it lasted. The popular thing
was to approve the anti-radical activities of the
American Legion. There was to be a performance of
"Old Heidelberg" in German at the Central Opera
House, but the Legion protested and it was called off.
William Howard Taft spoke on "Radicalism and the
American Legion" at a New York theater, approving
the organization's activities for upholding right
thinking. The eloquent barrister, Dudley Field

Malone, who had been a junior lieutenant in the Navy during the war, and also Collector of the Port of New York for a time, was denied membership in the Legion because he had taken the part of radicals.

Those were the days when Rose Pastor Stokes, the fiery Russian Jewess who had married J. G. Phelps Stokes, member of a wealthy old New York family, was being kicked around by police, Department of Justice agents and conservative orators. She spoke at a mass meeting in Manhattan Lyceum and predicted that America would be bolshevized in spite of Palmer and all his men. The years brought tragedy to her: she was divorced, only a few of the old guard of Reds paid much attention to her, and finally in the early summer of 1933 she died in Germany of cancer.

This period, too, was the beginning of the bitter feud between William T. Manning, then rector of Trinity parish and later Episcopal Bishop of the Diocese of New York, and the Rev. Percy Stickney Grant, rector of the Church of the Ascension. Grant, liberal to the point of being pink, had compared the deported Reds with the Pilgrim Fathers, which made a great many very nice people angry. Dr. Manning, on the other hand, demanded the publication of the names of wealthy persons who were reputed to have made contributions of money to the Red cause. Manning won in the end. He became Bishop, and was in a position to forbid the marriage of Grant to Mrs.

Lydig, who had obtained a divorce on grounds not sanctioned by the church. Grant died of anemia; Manning built the Cathedral of St. John the Divine.

The anti-radical feeling, of course, was not confined to New York. The Western hero of the Socialists, Victor Berger, who had been denied a seat in the House of Representatives and then had been re-elected, encountered insults wherever he went. He was to have made a speech in Jersey City (that city has always been liberal except in the countenancing of night clubs and gangsters), but he was intercepted by policemen when he came within a block of the hall. The cops put him in an automobile and drove him to Weehawken, where they put him on a ferry-boat bound across the Hudson for New York. Berger lived a long time after that—long enough to serve in Washington for years and to gain the respect not only of his constituents but of many others to whom the memory of those early days became dim and somehow unbelievable. Even Carlo Tresca, the flaming Red, lived to be tolerated by the New York cops.

Even more remarkable, William Z. Foster, the brains of the big steel strike of 1919, was allowed to roam the country. From an official in the good graces of the American Federation of Labor, he changed to a Socialist and then to the boss Communist. But no one, in the late twenties, became very much excited about William Z. Foster. With the coming of the

New Deal, he seemed as dead, as much a part of a forgotten era, as Eugene V. Debs or Coin Harvey.

Red-baiting, in this historic time, was not the only sport of New York or the country. Miller Huggins announced that he had bought Babe Ruth for the New York Yankees, taking him away from the Boston Red Sox. Jack Dempsey was negotiating to meet the frail Georges Carpentier in a match for the heavyweight championship of the world.

Even Broadway still had its good points. John Drew had come back to the stage in "The Cat Bird." John Drinkwater made a nice speech at the Garrick Theater to members of the New York Drama League. Al Woods engaged Theda Bara, the motion picture vampire, to appear in a new stage play called "The Lost Soul," which turned out to be a very bad idea. Douglas Fairbanks was at the Rialto in "When the Clouds Roll By." Geraldine Farrar for the first time appeared in the title rôle of "Zaza" at the Metropolitan Opera House. Fokine of the Russian ballet arranged to perform at the same house. Leo Ditrichstein was in a new play, "The Purple Mask," at the Booth Theater. Alice Joyce and Fatty Arbuckle were the film headliners at B. S. Moss's Broadway Theater. Mabel Normand had just gone West to work on a picture called "The Girl with the Jazz Heart," and the cinema directors were busy with the picturization of "Judy of Rogue's Harbor," to star

Mary Miles Minter. Adele Astaire was dancing with her brother, Fred, in "Apple Blossoms," at the Globe, and there was a story about town that she didn't wear stockings. Maxine Elliott began a week's engagement in "Trimmed in Scarlet." Florenz Ziegfeld announced that he had engaged Lillian Lorraine for his new "Nine O'Clock Revue" and the "Midnight Frolic" on the New Amsterdam Roof. Not a bad town then.

The cost of living was terrific, but everyone appeared to have money. Eggs had been a dollar a dozen over the holidays and had dropped only slightly. More than eight hundred hospital patients in New York City had been without sugar for a week; the sugar famine was real. Flour was scarce, and the United States Grain Corporation rushed in a supply of Government flour made of soft winter wheat. Arthur Williams, Federal Food Administrator, insisted that things weren't so bad, and gave out figures to prove that a man could completely clothe his wife for $58, including dress, overcoat, hosiery, shoes and underwear. Mr. Williams, who may have known his groceries, was laughed at by many husbands.

People wouldn't work. Householders were hopeful when they read that boatloads of Scandinavian servant girls were arriving who would work for as low as $7 a week; they had been used to snooty maids who demanded at least $15 a week. Nurses were

scarce, and many towns all over the country shut
down their schools, not because they had no money
to pay their teachers, but because they couldn't find
enough teachers to work for the accepted rate of pay.

There was, clearly, blood on the moon. Something ominous was in the air. It was the beginning
of all those changes in the structure of impulses of
society which, in a far later period, led Herbert
Hoover to appoint the most productive of all his
many commissions—the Commission of Social Trends.

From Chicago, even then, came the alarm that
crime had increased 25 per cent in a year. Gerald
Chapman and Dutch Anderson were teaming up as
mail robbers. Thanks to those two geniuses of the
underworld, Jake and Leon Kraemer (the brothers
Kraemer invented the so-called can-opener for getting into safes, as well as other technical advances),
the professional yeggmen were setting out on a highly
profitable period. A few profound commentators
began complaining of the decline of ethics; people,
somehow, didn't seem to know right from wrong any
more. Divorce cases were up 50 per cent in one
year in New York County. James J. Walker, a
bright young man, had just been made Democratic
leader of the New York State Senate. A judge in
the Bronx said it was all right for a woman to smoke
on the street ("What do you think this is, Hicks-
ville?"). A rumor came from a mid-Western col-

lege that the students had thrown out their Bibles and replaced them with ouija boards. Hundreds of persons had died of poison whisky; prosecutors in wet cities said it was a shame and that the guilty sellers would be prosecuted, but many of the drys said it served the drinkers right, and that the sooner such people were killed off the better.

It was at about 11:30 on the night of the Sixteenth that an elderly man wearing a gray overcoat walked east across City Hall Park. His friends knew him as Filthy Phil, because he had been out of polite society so long that he could not utter a simple sentence that was not reeking with blasphemy or venery. He was cursing quietly but savagely—at the authors of prohibition and at the unfathomable caprices of Jehovah. Near the statue of Nathan Hale he encountered an acquaintance and together they crossed the park, traversed Nassau Street and went up one flight. There was a bar, a bartender, and glasses and red liquor. Outside was the blizzard; inside, Phil was at home. Always, he said, there would be places like this. He became very drunk.

IT WAS LIKE THIS

J IM BRINCKER'S Nepenthe Club (and that was not the real name of either the man or the joint) will be remembered by its habitués, or "members," as they were called, with an affection bordering on the maudlin. It was an honest place. While the big racketeers were plotting their strategy at Valley Forge and keeping the lamp of liberty glowing, Jim was attending strictly to the retail business. He ministered to the thirsts of men who were born to drink; he and a few others like him were the patriots of the period. If they had laid down, prohibition would have worked.

Merely because he was old enough to drink in Mouquin's, Jack's, Luchow's and Joel's before the war, and because he knows who Gambrinus was (which is something Jim Brincker never thought much about, not being much of a classicist) the eloquent Benjamin de Casseres passed the prohibition years in his beery garden of memories, lamenting always in fizzy prose that there was a blight on the land and that the old days were best. The late Frank Ward O'Malley, of the beloved kidneys, also recalled with salty nostalgia the robustious nights at Jack's, with Corse Payton and Wilson Mizner and Spanish Jack O'Brien and the

Irish bacon and the dawn coming up like the boom-
ing of distant cannon-crackers.

Very well. The old men pass on. De Casseres
passed at least one evening in Jim Brincker's. O'Malley never was there, and died in France without
knowing that here, in the peculiar fashion of a hangout run under the shadow of the gallows, was a spot
which had become, through the dreary years, a haven
for old men and young. Jim's was the best type of
stag speakeasy. Those who went there knew that
there were other places in New York somewhat like
it, and operated on the same honorable principles,
but they contended that anyone with any sense always came back to Jim's. Real happiness lay only in
coming home to the old Nepenthe.

Some day, with the persistent crusade of Alfred
E. Smith, Dr. Nicholas Murray Butler and Mrs.
Charles H. Sabin bringing the country very near to
the promised land, the real name of Jim Brincker can
be disclosed. But even now, with respectability only
around the next corner, he is technically an outlaw.
His homely little club is as illegal as a den of pickpockets. So he must be protected in print, just as he
protected himself through the years with the jungle
cunning of the smart bartender, and just as he protected his thousands of customers during the time of
the drouth.

Jim never left the booze business for a day. The

idea of prohibition was to him simply a sociological aberration, a strange, alien scheme thought up by freaks. He always dreamed of running a beer garden, but the "club" was more practical. In his period of operation he established himself as one of the soundest men in New York. He could, so far as anyone ever knew or suspected, be trusted with anything, anywhere, at any time. The man in a corner might not be able to trust his partner, or his favorite cop, or his bishop, but he could trust Jim Brincker.

The blight of prohibition, in 1920, found Jim tending bar in a corner saloon in the Forties, a place patronized by Broadway lawyers, opera singers, theatrical men, devotees of the racetrack, press agents and a few newspaper men. He had been back of bars for more than fifteen years. He was of German extraction. He learned patience during the war; and through the long evenings, pouring out drink after drink, he learned a lot about the people of New York.

He understood, too, the value of thrift. Once he had batted around the country, not caring what happened to him. When he decided to settle down in New York he was still distrustful of established institutions, especially banks. He had the habit of putting his savings into a tin can which he kept hidden, securely, he thought, under one end of the bar. One night he found that his whole $800 was gone. A sneaking porter had stolen it. Jim went into a berserk

rage, but a detective friend calmed him down and
helped him recover the money. Jim put his cash in
a good bank. He added to his account regularly, and
in 1920 he had a comfortable nest-egg.

The proprietor of the corner saloon was ready to
surrender in January, 1920. He was tired, and he
believed, with the cloddish school of thought so common then, that the prohibitionists had captured the
country forever. Jim bought the lease from the old
proprietor and told his customers that, for a time
anyway, he would remain open as usual. He did. At
first there were a few very messy raids. The dry
agents, new at the business, were trying to find themselves—and whatever else was lying around. There
also were a few zealots among those first agents who
insisted that the law was the law.

Jim always managed to smooth out his difficulties,
for there were always people who, either out of
friendship or for a modest fee, were willing to help
him keep out of serious trouble. Soon the profits,
even with the considerable amounts paid out to cir-
cumvent the law, were greater than they had been
before prohibition. Jim made some English inn im-
provements, put in some funny brass gadgets, and
the place boomed. He served good food and whatever in reason one wanted to drink.

For four perilous years he stuck it out. Then he
saw that a corner place wouldn't do. It was too pub-

lic, like running a counterfeiting press in Macy's window. The constant shakedowns, the ever-present
dread of trouble, and the threats of raids, began to
give the old fellow the fantods.

Then one day (this was at a time when people
thought a corner was made for a bank and not for a
saloon) the real estate manager of a bank walked
in and bought out the lease. A skyscraper was to go
up, with a bank on the first two floors. Jim pocketed
his $60,000 profit on the lease and said he guessed
he would have to close up.

Before he moved out, however, he already had
leased the back ground floor of an ancient, creaky
building half a block away. He installed his fixtures
and moved into what was to become the Nepenthe
Club. On the old corner the skyscraper went up,
the bank moved in, and Hoover and Coolidge were
in Washington. In 1930 the bank closed, and many
of the upper floors of the skyscraper were vacant.
Then things, after being very bad, got much worse.
But Jim and his Nepenthe Club in the next block
were still making ends meet.

There was still another consideration in the move
from the corner to the back room. Soon after 1920
great, ravening hordes of women began to discover
what their less respectable sisters had known for years
—that it was a lot of fun, if you liked it, to get
soused. All over New York these up and coming

females piled out of their hideaways, rang the bells
of speakeasies, wheedled drugstores into selling them
gin and rye, and even in establishments of great decorum begged their escorts for a nip from a hip flask.
It was all very embarrassing. Jim's corner place, although he tried to keep a reasonable amount of decorum, could not escape the howling, reeling and
raging termagants. Sometimes they would merely
fall down. Again they would beg for just one more
drink; Jim would let them have three, watch them go
to sleep and then pour them into a cab and send them
home. Or one of the triangle things, husband, wife
and the other woman, would decide to put on an act.
There was one lady, no better, Lord knows, than she
should have been, who wanted to fight when in her
cups. She was rangy, and tawny-haired, and thewed
like Stanley Ketchel. She could slug toe to toe with
any man weighing under 200 pounds.

All this foolishness worried Jim. He was, for all
the fact that he had once been practically a hobo, a
stickler for good taste, with a little dignity thrown
in if possible. When he opened the Nepenthe he announced that never, in any circumstances, would a
woman ever be allowed to set foot inside the door.
Many other saloon-keepers, at about this same time—
that is, men who cared more for smaller profits and
less trouble than quick big money—came to the same
decision. The women said that Jim was a dour old

curmudgeon, a heartless woman-hater, and all that, but he kept his promise.

Not only did no woman ever come into the Nepenthe, but Jim always seemed vaguely annoyed when one called on the telephone. Now, Jim was not a woman-hater, though his private life, if any, was something which he kept carefully guarded, not more than five or six hundred persons ever suspecting anything out of the way, but he backed away from trouble. A rowdy scene in which a woman was involved would throw him into a swivet from which he wouldn't recover for days.

Thus, founded on enduring principles, backed by a man of vision and character, the Nepenthe became a sort of monastery where a man, hag-ridden, beset by nightmares, tortured by the roar of far-off artillery, could retire to ponder, to smooth out the tangled web of his existence, and to conquer his soul with a firm headlock.

Into this retreat of peace and erudition and heart-quickening cheer came some of the most entertaining men in the country. Also among the customers were some of the most colossal bores ever set loose on a sprinkling of sawdust. But it should be remembered that Martin's, the Belmont bar, and even the old Knickerbocker had their quota of bores—champions among bores, bores beside whom the garrulous reiterators in Jim's place would seem positively sparkling.

The food in the Nepenthe was as sound as could be found in New York for the price, and one could gorge there for a dollar and a half. The stuff was slightly heavy and Germanic, but it was tasty and filling. The two chefs, even though their contract called for enough free rye every day to intoxicate ten ordinary men, knew their business. There were enough tables for eighty men, and sometimes, when business was good, the place was filled at lunch and dinner.

Twenty-four men could belly up to the bar without undue crowding, and in 1927 and for more than two years thereafter the line was sometimes two deep. Jim's profits were staggering. In one year he cleared, after all expenses, bad checks, bribery and charity, almost one hundred thousand dollars.

The chief bartender was a sterling veteran named Harry. He had, one would think from the record, everything that makes for success: he was a veteran of the Spanish-American War, a tolerant Republican, a collector of guns, a lover of the open road, a fisherman of great skill, a polished fellow to introduce to one's friends, and an expert on colds, chills and fevers. On analysis, however, it was evident that he had two great faults: (1) he was a Methodist, with the hidebound earnestness and the innate suspicion of a prohibitionist, and (2) he was too much of a paternalist. He feared liquor, women and carefree drink-

ing men. He took violent dislikes to certain customers. To others he gave too much advice, and others
he stopped from drinking when they were far from
unconscious. He was a great bartender, but when
business began to dwindle Harry went away mys-
teriously, took up a respectable business, and turned
his job over to an old chap from Alaska who had been
drink-pourer to the sourdoughs when Harry was
fighting flies in Cuba. The new bartender, a chap
of dignified bearing who only got drunk once a year,
was as nearly perfect as a bartender could ever be.
He was, they said, a little hard of hearing, but no one
ever could swear that this was true. He never had a
fight, never lost his temper, never raised his voice,
and when he stopped a customer's drinks he did so
firmly but without arousing anybody. He never
bored people with his stories and never handed out
gratuitous advice. He didn't care.

Jim Brincker stuck to the plain drinks. He had
some fine wines in his cellar, but he pulled them out
only on special occasions. The principal drinks were
ale, old-fashioned Martini, Manhattan and Bacardi
cocktails, and anything the gentlemen would have in
the way of gin, rye, bourbon and Scotch. Ladies'
drinks, such as side-cars and Alexanders and pink
ladies, were never permitted. Nor would they ever
make a Tom and Jerry or a mint julep or a Ramos
fizz. Too much trouble.

The strength of the Nepenthe, of course, lay in the moral fiber of Jim Brincker the man. Out of all the raffish battalions of gyps, ex-holdup men, clip joint experts, towel-swingers and cheap thugs who handled illegal liquor from 1920 on, Jim and a few others of his sort held on to their innately decent ideals. Indeed, as one dry year rattled into another, Brincker seemed to grow in stature and poise and character. He became more mellow, his judgments were backed by better reasoning, and he took on a certain sheen that made him a distinguished man of his times.

There was a common delusion, held during the prohibition years by many well-meaning people, that all bootleggers, all keepers of such places as the Nepenthe, were friends of the prohibition law. Jim Brincker made money, but he had his headaches. He was, like so many others, a law-abiding citizen at heart. He would no more have swindled anyone, or forged a check, or connived at the robbing of a bank, or borne false witness against a neighbor, than he would have shot down babies with a machine-gun or slipped a customer a Mickey Finn. He liked to run a place where gentlemen came to drink and talk and eat, and that was all there was to it. He would much rather have done it legally, and before he dies he probably will do it with the full approval of the United States Government.

He had to be friendly with the police and the pro-

hibition agents. Indeed, some of these fellows had
been his friends, either as brother Elks or cops, long
before there was such a thing as prohibition. He
worked out his own code in dealing with them. The
three patrolmen who covered the block at various
hours got a regular retainer, as well as free drinks in
moderation—and the police were always moderate.
Prohibition agents were harder to deal with. The
agents were for the most part lazy. They passed a
lot of time in Jim's place, sitting and talking, instead
of being out drying up the town. Most of them,
however, were fairly decent fellows, and their de-
mands on Jim were never extortionate.

It was when a new squad of agents, or a new administrator, came to town and upset the machinery of enforcement that Jim had his worries. One day two
strange agents came in and announced that they were
going to raid the place. Jim talked and talked, and
finally the agents agreed to lay off for one thousand
dollars. For six hours Jim sat with them in a corner,
wheedling, arguing and appealing to their better na-
tures. Finally he went to the cash register, pulled out
fifty dollars and sent them on their way. They never
bothered him again.

One afternoon a squad of policemen burst into the
place, and they seemed pretty angry. Jim met them,
treated them courteously, gave them each a drink,
and got down to business. He had no trouble.

"Hell!" said the leader of the squad.   "I didn't
know it was this sort of a place.   I thought we were
raiding a poolroom.   Just tell the boys not to place
any more bets on the horses over the phone.   We
don't mind the regular business."

On another occasion two city detectives, who apparently had been drinking more than enough to clear
their brains, broke into the place and, with loud and
picturesque profanity, announced that they were
going to arrest Jim along with his bartenders and
waiters, as well as wreck the house.   Jim at once
brought all his conciliatory powers to bear on the
problem, but for a time it appeared hopeless.   Finally
he got the names of the two men, and from something they let slip he decided that they had mistaken
his place for another.

"Get out of here!" he roared.   "Your language is
too rough for this place.   Clear out or I'll call Captain —— and he'll throw you out."

The two raiders realized the enormity of their mistake and backed out with apologies.   Jim could nearly
always handle them.   Only once, so far as old customers remember, was he genuinely perturbed, and
in the circumstances no one could blame him.   There
were only a few men at the bar on that cold night in
the winter of 1927.   No one expected trouble.

The doorbell rang, and the waiter admitted three
men without questioning.   The three strode back to

the bar and ordered drinks. Strangers had come into
the place before, but these men were different. They
were powerfully built fellows, and they exuded a
sinister arrogance. All were dressed with exaggerated
elegance, and one of them had an Adolphe Menjou
mustache. All conversation stopped. Everybody felt
vaguely uncomfortable. One was sure, without being
told, that all three were dangerous and that they carried guns.

They had all the drinks they wanted, without offering to pay for them and without being asked for the
money. Then they told Jim they wanted to see him
alone. Jim, his face white and set, took them down
in the basement, to a little place back of the kitchen
where he sometimes invited some friends for card
games. They sat down at a little table and spread
their paws across the red and white checked tablecloth.

Upstairs, at the bar, a few of the customers decided to leave. The others talked but little. What
was happening to Jim? After a time the men came
back from the basement. The three strangers went
out and Jim came back to the bar. He volunteered
no information. He merely poured himself a drink,
stared dazedly about him, and then went into the
most quietly savage line of invective ever heard at
that bar. There was something in the quality of his
remarks which forbade further questioning, and no

one ever mentioned that evening, and the strange
visitors, again. The best guess was that they were
among the leaders of a mob of big bootleggers which
operated in Brooklyn, Providence, Boston and Atlantic Highlands, New Jersey—specifically, the group
which had among its principal brains such men as
King Solomon and Al Lillien, both of whom were
murdered in 1933. But what did they want? Cash?
An interest in the place? To force Jim to buy their
booze? No one except Jim knows. All the customers know is that the scene was as coldly terrifying,
and as bizarre, as if Alphonse Capone, Jesse James
and Gerald Chapman should appear unexpectedly
among the scholarly old gentlemen gathered at the
Century Club bar. Those who knew and admired
Jim Brincker always had sworn that his courage was
without limit, but this time, and with good reason,
he had been shaken to the core of his gizzard.

Jim was usually helpful to everybody. Other
speakeasy proprietors, old friends of his, often came
to him for advice and aid on matters of policy in running their joints. When one of these old chaps was
in hard luck, or dying of some occupational disease
such as tuberculosis or cirrhosis of the liver, Jim
would take care of him. He paid bills, arranged the
funeral and saw that a decent obituary got into the
papers.

One of his fixed ideas was that a place with both

good liquor and good food should not be too cheap.
High prices not only gave tone to a place, but they
enabled the proprietor to have a reserve fund for use
in case of business difficulties or trouble with the law.
One afternoon, on a clear warm June day, a friend of
Jim's put him and two other men in a big automobile
and bade them go with him over to a place in the New
Jersey hills, where, he said, they would have food
and wine and re-create themselves in the open air.

The place in New Jersey was a paradise—an old
Colonial house set among the trees and shrubs a half-
mile from the main road. It was late afternoon when
they got there. They had cocktails and then sat down
to a long and filling dinner, cooked by a genius among
Italians. The man who ran the place raised or made
most of his own stuff—applejack, wine, chickens,
milk, vegetables and what not. Along about nine
o'clock, when the four guests were surfeited, the
waiter brought the check. It was for $12 for the
four.

Jim flew into a dreadful rage. He told the waiter
to call the manager. Frightened, the waiter went out,
found his boss out in the garden and brought him to
the table. The manager, thinking Jim was complaining that the bill was too high, immediately began explaining how the expenses of the place, the
overhead, the cost of materials and heaven knows

what else, forced him to charge the amount on the bill.

"Hell!" snarled Jim. "That's not the point. You're crazy, and if you keep on this way you'll go broke. You can't give us a dinner like this, with all the drinks we've had, for $12. Man, you'll be bankrupt inside of six months. Why, this dinner bill ought to come to at least $24."

Then Jim did some figuring on the tablecloth to prove his point. They left the proprietor of the inoffensive little roadhouse shaking his head and wondering at the strange ideas of this New Yorker who apparently knew more about how to run his business than he did.

And Jim did know how to run a speakeasy. He could have run a big store, a manufacturing plant or a hotel of 1,000 rooms and 1,000 baths. He was, to be sure, fortunate in his clientele, which was drawn from widely different professions and businesses. This lucky circumstance was of enormous value. A man can live a fairly complete life in New York without having to go out into God's clean sunlight at all; likewise, in Jim Brincker's joint, it was possible to attend to all manner of business, and live a pretty full sort of life, without leaving the place at all.

If Jim didn't know, he could put you in touch with someone who did know about almost every hu-

man need. At the bar in one evening there might be
seen an undertaker, a florist, a family doctor, an eye
specialist, a ticket broker, a railroad executive, a lawyer, a banker, the head of a milk company, the boss
of a powerful labor union, a manufacturing stationer,
a civil engineer, a stage designer, a wholesale tobacco-
nist, a prize-fight promoter, a theatrical producer, a
vaudeville comedian and various members of national,
state and city officialdom who could give sound advice on everything from income tax returns to automobile license plates. Talking to these men through
the years gave Jim an amazingly wide range of
knowledge. It also made him a bit cocky, especially
when he had a few drinks in him, and he would want
to bet with argumentative customers. Who was on
the ticket with Bryan in 1908? How many square
miles in Australia? How much beer was made in the
United States in 1912? Which leg did Sarah Bern-
hardt have amputated, and was it above or below the
knee? How many were hanged for the Haymarket
riots? How many Jews are there in New York?
These are the matters that agitated the speakeasies
during prohibition years. Some issues could be settled by recourse to the World Almanac, others had to
be arbitrated, and still others were made the subject
of long and painful research by trustworthy experts.

Jim Brincker, as tolerant paternalist, was in the tradition of the great saloon-keepers of pre-prohibition

America. He granted to every man the right to cook his brains with whatever potion he preferred, but to a confirmed brandy drinker he would say, "For God's sake, drink something else now and then." Jim regarded Scotch-and-soda as the best of drinks. He warned customers away from his powerful Manhattans, and he would quietly point out the ultimate deadliness of the habit of drinking whisky sours to settle the stomach. There were, among the patrons of the place, three or four commuters who, when left to their own devices, would likely as not end the night in the wrong county, or even the wrong state. To these, when he saw they were beginning to bob and weave, Jim would say firmly, "You're catching the 9:13 for Speonk." If they doubted him, Jim would put on his hat and top-coat and escort them to the station.

Places like Jim's always have been havens of solace for widowers, for bitter men who were crossed in love in their youth, and for aging bachelors who would rather drink than waste their time at the annual Lonely Hearts' Ball (there was such a ball, run by Bernarr Macfadden's now dead *Graphic*). Such men are the best customers a saloon can have. Usually they are solvent and calm, and they have a quiet dignity foreign to most men who still have women folks to worry about. Jim had an eye out for their health, and his predictions of death had a ghoulish accuracy about them.

"That fellow will be dead in six months," he would say of a failing customer at the other end of the bar. He could tell by the pallor around the gills, the droop of the jaw, or the painful hunch of the shoulders. Being a realist, he knew that drink, certainly in the vast majority of instances, was responsible neither for the disease nor the final taking off. So he was patient and thoughtful with those old codgers who he knew would be in their graves, and with infinite tactful care he would supervise their diets. Then one day a regular customer would fail to come. Another day would pass, and another, and Jim would inquire. Then he would visit the hospital, and come back to mutter gravely around the bar about the inevitability of death, and to reaffirm the eternal truth that no matter who you are, or what you do, Charon gets you and takes you for a ride in the end. He would look at his own graying hair in the mirror, and fondle his flabby colorless cheeks, for he was a vain man at heart, and soon, when the first flush of sadness had passed, he would be laying plans for taking a group of children from an orphanage to the circus, or to Coney Island, or to some such place.

The general esteem in which Mr. Brincker was held during the prohibition era was shared by his own employees: the great Harry, who quit as bartender when the business slump became serious; Fred, the Alaskan veteran who succeeded Harry; Gus, the blond German bus boy who worked up until he became chief assistant to Fred; Adolph, the bald-headed waiter who used to be a wrestler, but who turned square because he got tired of having bigger men bang his head on the floor; Franz, the other waiter, who had a remarkable record as an infantryman with the German army during the war, and whose little body bore a dozen ghastly scars; the two unidentified monsters down in the kitchen, who guzzled and cooked day and night; and little Bill, the Negro porter, who was a man of high repute and a deacon in one of the largest Negro churches in Harlem. Bill had been with Brincker for years, swore by him, and in turn Brincker had entrusted Bill with as much as $25,000 to carry from one end of New York to the other. These are the only men Brincker had working for him during the long years the Nepenthe Club was in business, except for a few times, when a great uprush of business would make it necessary to call in three or four extra emergency waiters, usually friends of Adolph or Franz. For these lives Jim felt a deep responsibility. When, infrequently, one of them got drunk, he would fire him with a scarifying torrent of abuse, but in a few days the erring one would be back at work.

Other bars sprang up, made mistakes, had too many raids, and died. Jim's place, and many others some-

what like his, stayed on and on. In all truth it was a
better place than most of the old-time saloons. It
was pleasanter, for one thing, and it was inevitable
that it could go on for so many years without piling
up some romantic traditions of its own. Does anyone remember much about the old Knickerbocker
bar except that Maxfield Parrish's painting of Old
King Cole hung above it? And the Waldorf bar is
remembered chiefly because of some pointless garru-
lity attributed to John W. Gates, Tom Ochiltree and
other boresome coots of a long-vanished era. Jim
Brincker's place? Well, here are some of them,
picked from an endless list:

The night Sport Herrmann of Chicago blew into
New York, came into Jim's for dinner, and later ex-
hibited his gnarled and broken old hands, with their
scars and twisted joints, and told the appalling saga
of his boyhood hardships.

The night four detectives from Police Headquarters, waiting until 3 A.M., the zero hour for raiding a
place in Hell's Kitchen that was known in the patois
of the era as a "clip joint," passed the time in Jim's,
with the head of the squad delivering a lecture on why
a policeman is a better judge of the amount of evil in
a prisoner's heart than all the prosecutors and judges
on earth.

The night a professional arranger of big society
funerals told the story of the last days of a prominent

Newport gentleman, of how he used to read his morning mail while sitting out in the ocean and then tear
it up and throw it gleefully to the waves, and the
grotesque details of the final obsequies.

The night Jim gave a big dinner in his place for a
visiting member of the Department of Justice staff
from Washington. He served Dubonnet cocktails,
sauterne, Pommard, liqueurs and, much later, Scotch
highballs. The guests included three prohibition
agents, two wholesale bootleggers, two proprietors of
other speakeasies and two unidentified men of importance. They agreed that Jim was "the greatest
guy in the world," as who, in the circumstances,
wouldn't?

The night a brilliant young man, who had been
drinking brandy steadily for years, was asked by the
bartender why he ever started drinking in the first
place. "To forget a woman," said the young man.
"And now I keep on drinking because I can't think of
her name. I'm trying to remember who I was trying to forget."

The annual spring bet, made by Jim Brincker, that
there were more white horses than red-headed women
on a course from Fifth Avenue and Forty-second
Street down to the Battery and back up the West
Side. Six men, including the bettors and the um-
pires and watchers, would pile into a cab and pass the
afternoon counting horses and women. Jim always

won, for he knew that along the West Side docks and warehouses there were an enormous number of white horses.

The night of the great embarrassment, when an old fellow of extremely dignified bearing, who had been coming into the place for two years and boring everybody with his opinions on the innate soundness of the Hoover administration, was recognized as a man who had served a term in Sing Sing prison for larceny. Everybody felt pretty bad about this.

The night that a Swedish Count, who had been attending a performance at the Metropolitan Opera House, came to Jim's place during an intermission and was so charmed by the proprietor and his surroundings that he deserted his party and passed most of the next few days and nights discussing life with Mr. Brincker, with whom he later kept up a correspondence. The Count is the man suspected of caving in the chest of a set of stage armor with his bare fist just to prove it was not the real thing.

The night news came of the death of the silent man of mystery, who for eight years had been coming into the place every hour, taking one drink and walking out without speaking to anyone. He had averaged at least eight drinks a day for years. No one knew who he was until he died and left a considerable fortune.

And there were others: the former Major of en-

gineers who always enraged Adolph by calling him
"steward"; the gray-haired man called "Judge" who
was not a judge but who had a knack of frightening
policemen; the friend of Jimmy Walker's who left
the place forever after being rebuked by the bartender
for matching $5 bills; the wealthy Texas oil man
who amazed everybody with his diamonds and silk
shirts; the critic who, coming into the place for the
first time, was recognized by Brincker and brought
into a five-hour discussion of the drama, on which
Jim was a sort of rough-and-tumble expert; the brilliant little lawyer, gray now, who once was up for
disbarment, and who, while sipping his Scotch highball, talked low and earnestly on the merits of recti-
tude and sobriety.

On the day in April, 1933, when 3.2% beer became
legal, Jim Brincker was forced to make one of his
great decisions. He knew that many of his customers
liked good beer; he knew also that 3.2% beer was not
satisfying to the men who had been drinking his
Canadian ale and his hard liquor. Moreover, he suspected that if he took out a license to sell the weak
brew he would be subjected to a system of inspection
which would pile one more annoyance upon all his
other troubles with dry agents, policemen, building
and health inspectors. That, he figured, would mean
more bribery, very little revenue, and all sorts of possible trouble. So he decided to stick to being an out-

law, with the hard stuff, and to hope that not all his customers would desert him for the legal beer.

There was, too, another consideration, which was strong with Brincker, with many others of his position, and with a vast army of drinking men who demand hard liquor when they want it. Jim's fury against prohibition was honest. He could not understand why he should be told to sell only 3.2% beer when he knew that he and his customers preferred stronger beer. So he set his face against compromise, began perfecting his defenses against the new army of inspectors, extortioners, fixers and snoopers, and looked with as dubious an eye as ever on the strange workings of government. He will sell hard liquor until he is dead, or in jail, though he will hope for absolute repeal. For Jim is a patriot, and he fought for the rights of man when man, apparently, had no rights.

SNOOPERS AND AX-MEN

THE speakeasy and the night club made New York the heaven of the swinish prohibition agent. Other towns might have their good points, their lucrative graft and comfortable living, but New York, the wet, the wicked and the wealthy, was where all the snoopers hoped to go before they died. Some, alas, had to pass the prohibition period nabbing sellers of white mule in the oil towns, moonshine in the Southern hills and the dreadful assortment of foulsmelling poison which was bootlegged in the prairie states.

In New York the agent could walk less than a block from his headquarters before setting out to dry up the town, and get a wonderful meal and all he could drink for nothing—at any one of several places. It became the custom of these indolent fellows to establish certain protected hang-outs all over the city, places where they forced the proprietor to pretend that they were welcome, and to use them as a base for operations. It was a common sight in certain New York speakeasies to see a group of agents enter a place at noon, remain until almost midnight, eating and drinking, and then leave without paying the bill.

The dry agent, not alone by the intrinsically unpopular nature of his calling, but by his duplicity, his
bad manners, his cheapness and his occasional brutality, made himself the symbol of all that was wrong
with the law. The honest speakeasy proprietor, who
served good food and sound liquor, might pretend to
be on good terms with these guzzling, insatiable visitors, but once they turned their backs he would
gladly point out that, however low the lowest petty
grafting policeman might be, he was not as low as
the average prohibition agent. This is not to say that
there were not some decent men, conscientious workers, among the dry forces, but there were enough of
the high-binders to give the Federals the reputation
which they will have for many a year after the Eighteenth Amendment is buried. For a long time the
memory of those shake-downs will rankle in the
hearts of thousands of bartenders who were harassed
during the years of the great blight.

Consider how the raiding began in New York. It
was in January, 1920, that an agent went into Jack
Dunston's famous old restaurant in Sixth Avenue at
Forty-third Street and asked for a drink. He got
one. Then he asked for a half-pint of whisky and
got that, whereupon he arrested the waiter and the
captain and carted them off to jail. Now (and this
is something neither the agents nor the prohibitionists could ever understand) such a raid was resented

because Jack's place was anything but a vicious resort. Indeed, it was so respectable that Mr. Dunston
was a prominent citizen. And Mr. Dunston was
raided again, forced out of business. He died leaving
a tradition, and no one more than he would have
appreciated the end of prohibition.

The kindly, gruff and doughty James H. Moore,
who operated, and still operates, Dinty Moore's restaurant in West Forty-sixth street, was raided in
about the same manner—a manner which lacked all
sense and all finesse. Moore, who never tolerated
drunks, and who always took a great pride in his
food, for which he charged plenty, was annoyed by
the Federal agents off and on for years. At one time,
indeed, part of his place was padlocked.

All these early raids were dull. The first bit of
liveliness was introduced when the Rev. John Roach
Straton, with a snooper, went to Healy's and asked
for Scotch whisky. The joke was that at the ensuing
trial his testimony was adjudged incompetent because
he admitted he wouldn't know Scotch whisky if he
tasted it.

The real fun began with Izzy Einstein and Moe
Smith, two incredible creatures who had been sworn
in to help bring on the great drought. After a slow
start, feeling their way around, they opened up.
They raided all manner of places, using an amazing
variety of tricky devices and impersonations. Some-

times they were longshoremen, then scientists, musicians, icemen, swimmers and salesmen. Izzy and Moe lasted a long time and then left the service for reasons which have never been explained with complete frankness by either Izzy, Moe or Uncle Sam—all three splendid fellows.

This was the primitive period of raiding. The agents would raid any old place suspected of having liquor, arrest the owner, waiter or bartender, and then prepare to do it all over again in a few days or a few weeks. The error, of course, was in trying to close the outlets of booze. Places selling liquor multiplied; if there had been ten times as many agents their work would have been almost as ineffectual.

Ralph A. Day, boss of the agents in 1922, got the idea that it might help to raid the big places, to search for distilleries, and to find truckloads of alcohol on the way to the mixing and cutting plants. So they looked upstairs at Jack Dunston's and seized $100,000 worth of liquor, and Jack's trial in Federal Court was one of the first big liquor shows. All of the seized booze was brought into court on trays; this was in the days before a test tube was sufficient to satisfy a judge.

The raiders gained momentum and courage. E. C. Yellowley, billed as a man of indomitable will and unshakable tenacity, with a nose like a divining-rod for hidden spirits, came out of the moonshine regions of the Southern mountains with his "Flying Squadron." R. Q. Merrick, later to be zone chief, an experienced hand in rooting out booze, came along with Yellowley. In January, 1923, the scourge began; it looked serious for a time, but in retrospect it was only one of many similar drives, which accomplished little except the annoyance of a lot of people who wanted to see liquor, and others who wanted to drink it. Up and down town they went. In Greenwich Village alone they hooked twenty-five places.

Meanwhile New York State, whose Legislature was under the domination of upstate Republican drys, decided to take a hand by passing the state enforcement act known as the Mullan-Gage law. A long-forgotten man named Morris G. Markland (the law itself, soon repealed, also is almost forgotten) divided the city into three sections each patrolled by a platoon. Raids for a time were performed quietly and with a minimum of trickery or legal flummery. Owners of the land on which liquor was sold were handed summonses.

Then Richard E. Enright, New York's Police Commissioner, decided to put his finger into the mess. Suddenly all night resorts of the more populous variety found patrolmen in them, with all the police officials denying knowledge of what it was all about. In more than one place patrolmen were known to sneak up on a man who was about to drink some-

thing out of a teacup and smell the contents; one cop
in the Moulin Rouge sneezed in such a cup, which
was adjudged by one and all as bad manners. The
resort-keepers were frantic. They said they tried
to keep their waiters from selling liquor, but that if
the men chose to break the law the restaurants should
not be held responsible. Then came one of the first
real protests against methods of obtaining evidence;
it was disclosed that in some instances Federal agents
had induced civilians carrying liquor to accompany
them into restaurants.

In August of 1923 it was announced that hence-
forth no arrests would be made on the spot, but evidence would be taken along and personal injunctions
would be issued against offenders to restrain them
from any further violations. Then, when cases had
accumulated, the whole batch would be presented to
a United States commissioner. But the raids went
right on, and at about this time the eaters and drinkers of the city began asking what the hell? When the
agents raided Peter's Blue Hour in West Forty-eighth
street in September the patrons threw chairs, hard
rolls and wet spaghetti.

The New Year's Eve which ushered in 1924 was
wet and noisy. There were three raids—Gallagher's,
the Peek Inn and the Metamora Club. The Metamora once had been the Pre-Catalan, scene of glori-
ous, insane brawls by the free spirits of the early F.

Scott Fitzgerald period from the campuses of New Haven, Cambridge and Princeton. With the New Year came the saddest of all the yelps from the old line of restaurant-keepers. Ben Riley, inventor of the triple-sized cocktail glass which is only one of his many claims to immortality, decided to move his Arrowhead Inn farther uptown, to Riverdale, where rents were cheaper. Paul Henkel, of Keen's Chop House, Fred Muschenheim, of the Astor, and other leaders of the Society of Restaurateurs complained that prohibition was ruining the art of cooking and eating; that it was wrong for drugstores to serve lunch and that the Chinese restaurant menace was getting serious. They were to repeat these sentiments for many a day.

Commissioner Enright and his men kept up their work. They arrested the great Jefferson Blount out in Harlem; at that time he was described simply as a waiter, but before the end of the decade he was to be known as one of the leaders in Harlem entertainment. Some of Enright's men, aping Izzy and Moe at their worst, dressed up to look as they thought college youths should look when out on a bat, and raided Brown's Chop House, across Broadway from the Metropolitan Opera House. It was believed at the time that this raid had been made by the police because of the decision of Judge Learned Hand in Federal Court

that prohibition agents could no longer make arrests
on night suspect raids.

During 1924 the methods of the agents became
more and more open to public criticism. In April
Samuel Kupferman, an agent, killed a man while trail-
ing liquor. His story was that he had posed as a bootlegger to gain the confidence of the rum hounds, and
then when they learned who he was they drew guns
and he had to shoot in self-defense. Kupferman's
story stuck, but it didn't help prohibition. The ten-
sion was relieved somewhat when a story came out
that a squad of dry agents, entering a vault in search
of liquor, had been attacked by rats. Somehow this
was regarded as being extremely funny. Then everybody laughed even more when Izzy and Moe had to
apologize for making a mistake in seizing some of
Col. H. H. Rogers's bonded pre-prohibition liquor.

In the spring of 1924 New York City was preparing to entertain the National Democratic Convention
at the old Madison Square Garden. There was a great
pother about drying up the city before the delegates,
most of whom were politically dry but wild for the
bottle in the big city, could gather for their quadren-
renial hippodrome. Six hundred padlock suits were
drawn up; many a little speakeasy was raided; agents
descended on drugstores which had been selling booze,
and some restaurants, run principally by Gil Boag,
Paul Salvin and their partners, got into trouble. It

made little difference to the liquor supply when the
thirsty Democrats arrived. Most of them stayed at
the old Waldorf-Astoria. Somehow, in spite of the
agents, liquor seeped into some of the rooms, and a
delegate who knew his way around could find plenty
to drink in a block's walk in either direction. While
Al Smith and William G. McAdoo were at each
other's throats in that long and bitter convention, the
delegates were able to get their liquor as long as their
money held out. Even so, the agents added to their
unpopularity during this period by creating scenes
in both the Waldorf and the Ritz-Carlton.

In August Robert J. Owens, an agent, made a grave
error. He swore out an affidavit against the wrong
place, raided it, and it turned out to be the home of a
man who had married the niece of Chief Justice William Howard Taft of the United States Supreme
Court. The liquor, pre-prohibition stuff which had
been bonded and held in a vault in the house, was returned to the owner. Mr. Owens was dismissed from
the service. Curiously, the Anti-Saloon League insisted that Owens should have been kept on the force
and that the man who owned the liquor should have
been punished—under what law, heaven only knows.

Then, in December, Judges Learned Hand and Au-
gustus Hand in Federal Court ruled that a night
search for liquor on a day warrant was illegal, and

vice versa, with the results that booze which had been
taken from scores of places had to be returned.

The agents at this time had done two things: they
had driven many liquor sellers into unventilated basements, where the customers were admitted after undergoing scrutiny through a peep-hole, and they had
given the opening for the operation of the night club
where butter-and-egg men (a common phrase used
in that remote time to describe free but undiscrimi-
nating spenders) could throw away all the money
they had.

In March, 1925, Emory R. Buckner, the new
United States Attorney for the Southern District of
New York, gave the city what was perhaps the most
thorough and conscientious of all attempts to enforce
prohibition. Before he took office he had spent $1,500
of his own money getting evidence against resorts.
His corps of bright young assistants, young lawyers
who had been out of college only a short time, gathered the evidence and then did their best to make
padlocks stick. In a few instances they were successful, and there was a damper on night life, chiefly
during the vacation season.

Mr. Buckner was a brilliant lawyer, a wet by conviction and personal preference, but he brought all his
great ability to his job, and he gave up drinking while
he was at it. Although to him it all appeared perfectly reasonable, New Yorkers to this day cannot

understand why such a man would risk the almost inevitable unpopularity. Among the first of his casualties were some famous names—Otto Baumgarten, who at the Crillon served some of the best food on earth, Larry Fay, the Club Borgo, the Beaux Arts and the Silver Slipper.

In that fall of 1925, however, Mr. Buckner came very near bagging some big game. It had been suspected for some time that large liquor syndicates were in operation, directed by men of remarkable cleverness, no matter how bad their police records might have been. In September, after careful research, Buckner's men raided the big organization headed by Waxey Gordon (also known as Irving Wexler or Wechsler) which had headquarters in the Knickerbocker Building. Among the twenty-seven men said to be in the conspiracy was Abe Greenberg, an old St. Louis thug, who more than eight years later was to be murdered in a hotel in Elizabeth, New Jersey.

This syndicate did at least $200,000 worth of business a month. It had secret codes, navigators' charts of liquor lanes from Nova Scotia, and all the paraphernalia of rum-running that heretofore had been believed to exist only in the imaginations of sensational writers. Buckner said it was the first blow at "the real Rum Row." There were records of single transactions for Scotch whisky amounting to $240,000.

What of it? Some of the group were inconvenienced for a few months, and then the case was forgotten. Waxey Gordon himself became the owner of hotels, breweries and distilleries, and it was not until 1933 that another United States Attorney, George Z. Medalie, began his prosecution on a charge of income tax evasion, a move which precipitated a bloody war in the underworld, with four government witnesses murdered in a few days.

And yet, the seizure of the Gordon organization, even if it didn't make much difference, pointed out the way to the brains back of prohibition enforcement. They argued, and sensibly, that the only way to dry up the country was to attack the source of supply, and for many years they held to this theory. The fact that it failed was not because the theory was wrong, but because the Government could not supply the staggering amount of money, the men and the intelligence necessary for the job.

The liquor gangs, the importers, the distillers and the brewers, began to use codes and radios. The Government conducted almost interminable attacks against distilleries and warehouses, though now and then reverted to the old system of raiding small restaurants and speakeasies.

Next came a man in whom the prohibitionists had great faith—Major Chester P. Mills, a former army officer, who was put in charge of enforcement in New

York. It was the same old story. Sometimes the agents used axes, sometimes they fought with dogs and monkeys, and sometimes they stooped to such idiotic performances as raiding a Jewish wedding party for wine just as the rabbi was in the midst of the ceremony. Major Mills won a prize from William C. Durant, the Wall Street speculator and automobile manufacturer, for a monograph on how to enforce prohibition, and in 1933 he was indicted by the Federal Government for allegedly taking part in an alcohol conspiracy.

The successor of Mills in this most difficult and amusing of all prohibition enforcement jobs was Major Maurice E. Campbell, a former reporter and press agent, who probably did more than any of his predecessors to enrage the populace. After leaving office he announced himself as a rabid anti-prohibitionist, but while he had the job he used all the tricks in the book to enforce prohibition.

As the Christmas holidays of 1927 approached, Campbell's raiders were busier than usual. On the night of December 29 his men wrecked Helen Morgan's night club and carried away the furniture without a warrant, a proceeding which, the Government contended, was legal under the provisions of the United States Revised Statutes, by which the property of one who has not paid the tax on liquor may be confiscated. This was a new wrinkle; although

Campbell said the raid and the procedure had been
ordered from Washington, it was said that after the
raid he was called to Washington and censured for it.

After the wet New Year's, the city, and most of
the rest of the country, soon became aware of the
presence in Washington of one of the most remarkable women of her time, Mrs. Mabel Walker Willebrandt, Assistant United States Attorney General.
She was described as "deft and inscrutable," and she
was at her best in 1928, the year in which night club
life, along with exciting raids and trials, reached its
most sublime flower.

Mrs. Willebrandt planned to discard the old technique of raiding and to work with new methods, and
with men of her own persuasion. She argued that
even a stupid night club hostess could spot the ordinary prohibition agent a mile away, a theory which
has some sense, as the man who looked the most like a
bum in any night club probably would be the agent.
The days of Izzy and Moe and their disguises were
ancient history. The new agent must be a good
spender, personable, entertaining, able to make friends
with even the most stand-offish night club proprietor,
man or woman.

As an example of the new trend in raiding methods,
there was the descent upon the Jungle Club on February 17 by the same gang of agents that had wrecked
Helen Morgan's place. This time the agents did

everything but apologize for making arrests; they took evidence seemingly with regret; in every respect they tried to behave with great urbanity. Moreover, this was the first raid in which women had been employed by the agents to accompany them— Mrs. Willebrandt's contribution to the advancement of the New Woman.

On the last day in February the Government, apparently disturbed by the bitter criticism stirred by the hatcheting of Helen Morgan's place, ordered all her· furniture returned to her and withdrew all charges. It was a victory for La Morgan, but the end was not yet, for Mrs. Willebrandt was determined to put the lovely, dreamy Helen out of business.

Moreover, in this spring of 1928 it was generally conceded that nothing could stop Alfred E. Smith from getting the Democratic nomination for President. Of all the many counts against Smith, one was that he was a New Yorker. As such, he was to be taken as the high and menacing symbol of evil and his name held up before the country as the man who represented all that was abhorrent about the great city —from pronunciation to liquor-drinking. Now, of all the Americans who became famous during the era of prohibition, few loved life more than Al Smith, but he never was a night club habitué. He was always a home boy, and his personal sympathies were with the more puritanical Catholic wing.

On the night that the sweating hordes at Houston,
Texas, had given Smith the nomination, the dry
agents in New York went into several clubs, seized
the liquor and turned the patrons out into the street.
Dr. James M. Doran, in charge of the agents in Washington, and Mrs. Willebrandt, the brains of enforcement, denied that there was anything political in the
timing of the raids, though they admitted sending
many special agents to New York to augment the
staff of Campbell. Among the places raided at the
time of the Smith nomination were Helen Morgan's,
for the second time, and Texas Guinan's.

By August it was announced that padlock proceed-
ings had been started against thirty-six Broadway restaurants and night clubs in addition to many individual prosecutions for selling liquor. Most of the
evidence had been obtained by agents sent to New
York without the knowledge of Campbell, and some
of these agents had their wives on the Government
expense account. Four agents came from Washington, two from Denver, two from Oklahoma, two
from Philadelphia, one from Kansas City and one
from Dallas.

One agent said he had been in Miss Guinan's place
twenty-three times, buying liquor each time. She
said he was a pest, and that he once sent her some
orchids which she gave to her girls. In Washington
Dr. Doran said these raids meant the end of the night

club, and some of the night club owners seemed to agree with him. Even Helen Morgan, who had had so much hard luck, said she was quitting. Of course it wasn't the end, and a year later it all seemed very futile and foolish in retrospect.

The agents spent from $25 to $42 for champagne, $15 a pint for brandy, $10 a pint for rye and Scotch whisky, and as high as $2.25 each for cocktails. It was estimated that the Willebrandt raids in New York cost at least $75,000. Judge Thomas Thacher, who later was to be Solicitor General of the United States, dismissed a great many of the padlock actions, and vacated others that already had been granted. Smith was beaten for President for a dozen reasons that had nothing to do with night clubs. Recapitulation: The agents had done more than all their forerunners to make New Yorkers hate prohibition; Mrs. Willebrandt had made herself extremely unpopular, a situation which she did not improve when she later became counsel for the California grape-growers and their silly wine bricks; the Government received only $8,400 in cash and fines; there were only fifteen convictions which carried jail sentences of from thirty days to six months, and no one of any importance whatever, either in the operation of night clubs or in the direction of big bootlegging enterprises, had anything pinned on him.

It was almost a year after the Government went

into action that Texas Guinan and Helen Morgan came to trial. Guinan, after a mildly amusing trial, was acquitted because she insisted that she was purely an entertainer and could not be tried for aiding and abetting a nuisance. Helen Morgan was freed without having to take the stand, although the judge had virtually ordered the jury to convict. The whole thing was a farrago of unprecedented nonsense, and the business of having fun in New York went on as usual.

At the beginning of 1929, with the Jones law in effect, and with 270 agents at his command, Major Campbell continued his efforts to stop drinking in New York. Day by day the reputation of the agents became worse; it was announced that in nine years of prohibition agents had killed 197 persons, and in each case the agent had been exonerated on his plea of self-defense.

After a moderately inactive year, Campbell rang down the curtain on the year 1929 by conducting nineteen raids on New Year's, making fifty arrests, none of them of any particular importance. It was in February, 1930, that the Major got another idea. Twenty-five agents raided the Hotel Manger (now the Taft) and Campbell said he would bring an equity action to padlock the entire hotel. The Cornish Arms also was raided. Campbell went further and announced that hotels must not sell accessories,

such as ginger ale, mineral water, ice or bottle open-
ers. The result of all this was next to nothing. No
hotel was padlocked, and, despite the incessant raiding in Harlem, Greenwich Village and the streets off
Broadway and Fifth Avenue, drinking continued.

After helping the police clean up some sellers of
poison liquor along the Bowery and the Brooklyn
waterfront, Campbell's men suddenly amazed everyone by raiding the Central Park Casino, arresting the
whole staff on a charge of selling "set-ups" into which
one might pour intoxicants. Some very nice people
were at the Casino and they were angry. Such a raid
helped to cheapen the Government, and to bring the
agents into lower esteem than ever, for at the Casino
no crime was being committed, no poison was being
dispensed, and it certainly was not the sort of place
where crooks foregathered to hatch their sinister plots.

In July Major Campbell got out of office, firing a
bitter blast at certain Treasury officials and at the
staffs of the local United States Attorneys. He was
all for repeal of the Eighteenth Amendment, and soon
started a crusading magazine called *Repeal*. He was
succeeded by Andrew McCampbell, as sober and
well-meaning a man as ever tried to perform the impossible. He had no liking for showmanship, as Major
Campbell had, and he did not accompany his agents
on raids. For many years he had chased moonshiners
all over the Southwest, and his reputation was good;

he was not only hired to enforce prohibition, but he believed in it. He said he had a free hand, but he made no promises. He merely intimated that he would attempt to dry up the sources of supply—the old dream again.

Under the McCampbell régime the agents, though hampered in their work by a constantly mounting pile of court decisions which cramped their freedom of action, did very little brutal ax-work, very little slapping of hip-pockets, a minimum of smelling glasses in restaurants, and less trickery on the small fry than had been practised under previous administrations. And yet the pattern was about the same.

The men raided breweries, cutting plants, distilleries, groups suspected of diverting alcohol, importers of French wines, sellers of bad booze, yachts suspected of carrying liquor, old breweries, cordial shops and malt stores.

McCampbell was inclined to continue the practise of using women to accompany agents on certain jaunts to obtain evidence, but his chief in Washington, Amos W. W. Woodcock, frowned on this practise. Even at this time the Government was beginning to cut down on the costly folderols of enforcement, and it cost money to take women along to night clubs.

Although there was no Mrs. Willebrandt this time, and Al Smith would not be nominated for President,

the early part of 1932 brought to its fullest development the system of raiding de luxe clubs and confis-
cating the fittings. In the great spring raiding festi-
val of 1932, just before the Democrats nominated
Franklin D. Roosevelt for President, there was an
enormous increase in arrests and padlocks over the
previous year. In spite of the constant sapping by
raids, graft and bad business, many of the clubs, and
even a few small speakeasies, had been fitted up with
stuff which ran into real money. Draperies, panel-
ings, mirrors, carpets, bars, paintings, the finest of
kitchen equipment—all these were seized by agents
to be auctioned off for the Federal Government. At
auction the prices were ridiculously low. The raided
clubs either opened up in the same place, or moved,
taking their patronage with them. About the only
result of all this hullabaloo was to make the owners
cautious in fitting up their new places; most of them
were afraid to spend much on decorations and gewgaws.

The last days of Mr. McCampbell had about them
a touch of genuine melancholy. The Democratic administration had reduced the number of agents and
their expenses, even going so far as to refuse to foot
the bills for agents who bought drinks to get evidence.
Mr. McCampbell, at best, got very little fun out of
life, and now it was seldom that he heard of a raid on
a night club. He remained in his office while his agents

wandered about the streets of New York, trying half-heartedly to spot places where deliveries of liquor were being made.

It was in the spring of 1933 that the proprietors of night clubs and speakeasies began to suggest to the agents who had been their guests over the years that it was about time they began paying for what they ate and drank. One resort owner told the agents that they could still hang around his place—though he had half a mind to boot them out—if they would pay for their liquor at wholesale prices. The agents agreed.

Even before the big cutting down of enforcement on July 1, 1933, the number of agents in New York City had been reduced to sixty-three, and virtually all of them were known by sight to hundreds of boot-leggers, night club owners, waiters, bellboys, bartenders and doormen. Not that their identity mattered much, for the agents had succumbed to a deep ennui; they didn't care any more, for the racket was as good as over.

With the agents so lazy that they rarely stirred from their favorite bars, with drugstores selling all the good prescription rye and bourbon that anyone wanted, and with 3.2% beer places opening up all over town, the owners of the higher class of speakeasies were worried more about economics than about the law. Many such places closed in the summer of 1933 to await the coming of whatever machinery might be set up after repeal of the Eighteenth Amendment. Business was so bad that great droves of dry agents, who might have been tempted to make a final shake-down tour before they were fired, desisted because there wasn't anything in the cash register.

Then, on July 1, good old Andrew McCampbell, who had seen it coming for weeks, picked up the telephone and got the news from Washington that he was to have a long, long furlough, along with a great many of his few remaining agents. It had been a sad few months. The Government had abolished, by withholding funds, the two most powerful aids to the raiding of the big booze organization—wiretapping and informers. Again, although it was easy for agents to observe drinks being served over bars, that was not enough. To obtain evidence for padlocking, the dry agent must prove, first, that he saw an amber-colored fluid served; second, that the fluid was a beverage containing more than the legal amount of alcohol, and, third, that the customer paid for the drink.

One of the last places raided by McCampbell's men before he quit office was the Club Richelieu in West Fifty-first Street, where two men were arrested charged with maintaining a nuisance. What his motive was, no one ever found out, for scores of other

clubs, differing little from the Richelieu, were operating all through that section of the city.

After McCampbell left, the skeleton force of agents
left under Administrator Hanson made a few raids
just to keep their hands in. One was on the Biarritz,
a rather exclusive place in East Fifty-second Street.
One of the agents resembled a college youth in his
white linen suit, and the other wore a pince-nez and
a brown, well-fitting suit. They went to the bar
on the second floor of the four-story building, were
refused drinks by a bartender who apparently recognized them, and then they went behind the bar,
seized nineteen bottles of liquor and arrested a bartender and a waiter. As they walked out with their
prisoners the agents caught another man bringing
twenty-four bottles of gin into the place. All three
prisoners were released in $500 bail each. No one ap-
peared to take it very seriously.

In the enforcement of prohibition—that is, the
actual control of the outlets of liquor—the New York
police, by and large, followed a more sensible policy
than the Federal agents. The police raided usually
only on specific complaints from persons who had
been robbed or otherwise mistreated, or from neighbors who objected to noise and other forms of annoyance. The police turned over liquor seized in such
places to the Federal authorities for prosecution.
What happened? Usually nothing happened.

In the course of the more than thirteen years which spanned the onslaught of the prohibition agents on New York City, the enforcers tried every trick in the book of rules, and, except in a few cases, they failed utterly to make an impression upon any of that great army of individuals who made it their life work to supply New Yorkers and visitors with liquor and entertainment. Toward the end, it was not the agents, but lack of customers, that worried the club owners.

How corrupt were the majority of the agents? It would be impossible to say without getting the detailed confessions from either the agents or the resort proprietors on whom they preyed. Certainly there were well-authenticated instances of fixed protection being paid over long periods, in addition to sporadic shake-downs from new agents. The most noteworthy exhibits found among the seized records of almost every large liquor distributing organization were lists of the names of prohibition agents who had been fixed—sometimes accompanied by another and smaller list of agents who were adjudged honest and beyond the reach of bribery or influence.

The agents kept up the price of liquor. Their extortions, their free drinks and free meals, forced the ordinary customer to pay twice what he should have paid for liquor. They were, in many instances, so brutal and boorish and grasping that even the sensi-

bilities of the lower class of speakeasy proprietors
were shocked—and some of these men are hard to
shock.   To be sure, some of them, beginning way
back with Izzy and Moe and ending up with some of
the old-time agents still left on the staff when Mc-
Campbell quit, were pleasant enough men, good to
their families and loyal to their friends.   As a class,
however, they made themselves offensive beyond
words, and their multifarious doings made them the
pariahs of New York.

FROM CABARET TO HOT-CHA

MOST of the genuinely great masters of entertainment of the pre-prohibition period are dead now, or, like George Rector and Jacques Bustanoby, are in quiet backgrounds. These men, together with such persons as John and Thomas Shanley and John Reisenweber, built their reputations on the solid foundation of good food and tasteful presentations. This type of night life, the cabaret period, began as far back as 1911, when the Brothers Bustanoby astounded everybody by giving dancing with supper.

The cabaret, during the war and immediately afterward, found the going tough. It was being smirched by a cheaper and less leisurely life, harried by the dance halls and chevvied by all manner of reformers, vice crusaders, licensing regulations and the massed forces of virtue. After 1919 they were hardly cabarets in the old sense, although the term continued in use until the late twenties.

It was impossible for these places, with their enormous real estate investments, their floors as large as armories, to withstand prohibition. They tell of a pathetic evening in old Shanley's, already moribund, when a guest asked for a steak with half a pound of butter sauce. "Why, sir," sighed the waiter, "if there was that much butter in the house Mr. Shanley would eat it himself."

The new night life came rapidly after prohibition. The night club was being born. Rector's became the Café de Paris, and the Folies Bergère entertained great hordes of people nightly. A man of vision named Jules Ansaldi gets most of the credit for the idea of combining the old high-class cabaret restaurant with a team of featured dancers, and to form a place with a restricted, exclusive membership.

During the first years of prohibition the Palais Royal had Paul Whiteman, the Moulin Rouge was in its prime, and there were the Bal Tabarin, the Beaux Arts Café, the old Little Club, the Montmartre, the Tent and Monte Carlo—all somewhat different from the old cabaret and at the same time different from the later night clubs. They were brash, prosperous, American. The managers of many of these places were of a different breed from such old-timers as the Shanleys, Reisenweber and Captain Jim Churchill; they were foreigners who knew little about cooking and didn't bother to learn, for their customers didn't care. The new children of the night wanted a gay show, swift dance music, and no curfew. Moreover, they were able to pay for what they got.

In keeping with the new demand for splashy entertainment, the Chinese chop suey establishments began moving uptown, and 1923 found them deep in the hearts of many who wanted dancing, a sort of show, and a dinner, all for a dollar and a half.

How innocent the old-time cabarets appear, viewed after the years of the hot night clubs! And yet these places had to contend with enemies almost as persistently annoying as prohibition agents and shakedown artists. There was a serious attack in 1915, when a committee headed by Mrs. Henry Moskowitz, who later was to become the chief confidential adviser of Alfred E. Smith, gathered much fearsome data against the cabaret. The object of this committee was not so much to abolish dancing as to divorce it from restaurants, and divorce both dancing and eating from drinking. It was dangerous, it appeared, to eat, drink and dance in the same place.

All this material was placed in the hands of George H. Bell, Commissioner of Licenses under Mayor John Purroy Mitchel, who invoked a one o'clock curfew against all restaurants selling liquor and having music and an entertainment. Only resorts holding club charters, and there were many of these, could admit "members" after the deadline. However, most of the "clubs" obeyed the one o'clock closing ruling.

Bell had reports from 125 special investigators in addition to the Moskowitz findings. The battle against evil was on. Rector's was fined $500 for presenting its revue without a license for a theatrical

performance. Reisenweber's, Maxim's, the Tokio and
the Pekin were fined within six months and the floor
show discontinued. It was a year later before a
higher court reversed the decision on the fines.

In 1916 the State Excise Board began an inquiry
into the methods whereby cabarets kept open under
ancient "club" charters, a pillowing by legal techni-
cality which was greatly resented by the restaurant
men. On top of these troubles inspectors turned in
a report on 257 restaurants, rating the food in only
one place as "good."

Then came a short revival late in 1916. A place
called Les Fleurs opened in West Forty-fifth Street,
with a Meyer Davis orchestra and Clifton Webb and
his partner to dance. There was a novel "reserva-
tion charge" of $2 to insure "a high type of clientele."
While performing at this resort Webb invented a
dance called "London Taps," which served to remind
the rounders that a war was going on in Europe.
Rector's, always hopeful, announced great plans for
1917, with a Hawaiian orchestra from the musical
show, "Seven Chances," to entertain the guests.
Reisenweber's opened a new ballroom, decorated by
Joseph Urban in gilt at a cost said to have been
$250,000.

This was all pretty blatant, and soon John F. Hylan,
the Mayor-elect, and District Attorney Edward
Swann announced that, beginning January 1, 1918,

there would be a lot of cleaning up. With the war
on, the bans already were rigorous. No drinks could
be sold to service men, and none to women accompanied by service men unless a male civilian was in
the party. Pep speakers and patriotic societies
damned the cabaret as being wasteful, even sinful,
and "lobster palace" became a phrase to hiss. Next
came a twenty per cent tax on all receipts. It was
tough business. Some of the old places began closing
even before July 1, 1919. Louis Sherry, worried
about prohibition and "social unrest," said he was
going to stick exclusively to the catering business.
Downtown Mouquin's, at Ann and Fulton streets,
held out for six months and then closed, and the smiling Emile with his wine card was no longer about his
pleasant duties. Old Henry Mouquin, from his re-
tirement among his white oxen in Virginia, had issued
a famous bull: "Never will we raise the price of our
wine; our food, yes—the wine, never!" He never
did. The blight was coming. Grain was to take the
place of the grape. Cramped lechery was to supplant
the old mellow spaciousness.

It may be that the purveyors of the old type of
entertainment lacked vision. Most of them were
staid men, had been in business for years, and were
completely befuddled by the problems brought about
by prohibition. They couldn't untrack themselves.

During the first three years of prohibition they took
a terrible beating from the Federals.

Uptown Mouquin's, which had opened in 1897,
was raided; the officers of Maxim's ran afoul of the
prohibition law; the agents found enormous quantities of booze upstairs at Jack's; even poor old Tim
Shine, mouselike and taciturn, suffered the seizure of
much liquor upstairs in his Seventh Avenue place, at
which he sneaked away and passed the whole prohibition era practically incognito in a hideaway in
Forty-ninth Street; Reisenweber's was raided, forced
into two small rooms, and finally driven out of business; William Ockendon (Billy the Oysterman) was
raided but he stayed in business, and so did James
(Dinty) Moore, whose restaurant actually was en-
larged and improved during prohibition, which was
almost miraculous; agents raided the Blue Ribbon,
and rough ax-men got after Janssen ("Janssen wants
to see you").

The hotels began to adopt the table d'hôte, long the
symbol of the red-ink joints, which were being driven
to the wall. The cover charge, finally held by the
courts to be legal, had the customers puzzled. Some
thought it was to pay laundry and linen expenses;
others regarded it as a sort of tip, and still others
thought it was to pay rent or insurance. S. Jay Kauf-
man kicked about a fifty-cent cover charge at Don

Dickerman's Pirate's Den in the Village, but the judge threw the case out of court.

At the end of 1923 most of the old places were gone. Even Murray's Roman Gardens, of which it was said when it opened in 1909 that it "reproduced the appurtenances of Ancient Rome in all their original glory," had to close, and so did the Knickerbocker.

The real night clubs began to reach their full development in 1924, when they began springing up around town in great profusion. There was nothing crude about most of them, except the manner in which they extorted money from their guests. Some of them were run by high-toned people and were exceedingly swanky. A group of women of society, with the aid of famous artists, opened the Lido-Venice in East Fifty-third street, one of the better types of resort. Other smart clubs of this period, where the food was good, were the Mirador, the Moritz and the Deauville.

There were other sorts—all sorts. Larry Fay, the horse-faced racketeer, opened El Fey and Fay's Follies, with Texas Guinan as an entertainer. She greeted customers with her cheery "Hello, sucker," and the customers seemed to like it. Fay soon went bankrupt, but his place hummed while it was going good. If a man wanted to throw away a lot of money, and a great many men appeared to be obsessed with this idea at the time, Fay's club was an almost perfect place to do it. A speakeasy proprietor who knew Fay tells this story:

"I had just bought a big lot of liquor from Larry for my place when I heard he was opening up his night club. I got a few of my friends together and we went up one night. You know, I wanted to give Larry a play. He was a pretty good sort of guy and I wanted to see him prosper. Well, we drank every-thing—champagne at $20 a quart and all that. Larry sent me the bill the next day. It was $1,300 for the evening for me and my four or five friends. But I was glad to pay it. It was worth it. I had a hell of 'a good time."

The night club had a curious and diverse appeal. To some it was a sex-exciter. To others, frequenting a night club and throwing away money was a form of exhibitionism. Then, too, a great many Amer-icans, New Yorkers included, always have had only the most vague and elementary notions of what con-stitutes a good time. Wealthy men from out of town visited the clubs for appalling orgies of spending and drinking, and most of them seemed to think it was worth the cost. One broker, who later went to Sing Sing prison after he had wrecked his firm, ex-plained that during the boom period he spent hun-dreds of dollars a night in the clubs and found that it paid by bringing him new customers. Also, there

was the staid home boy, who lived with his family
out in Queens County, but who, for some reason that
lies buried in the inscrutable places of the human
mind, embezzled, over a period of many years, more
than $60,000 which he spent in night clubs. The
probation report on this ordinary competent and
sensible fellow, who had stolen from the banking firm
which employed him, discloses that he usually went
to the clubs alone, that he rarely drank to excess, and
that the money went principally as payment to singers. This fellow would pay as much as $100 to hear
a loud-mouthed woman in a night club (a woman
who meant nothing to him whatever) sing his favorite song, "Mother Machree."

The crooks began to enter the business. Larry Fay
himself, who had a record of forty-six arrests, was
no vestryman, but he was infinitely better than many
others. At its best the night club, in all sense, was a
poor imitation of the old-time spacious, clean-aired
cabaret; at its worst it was horrible—a hangout for
thugs, cadets, porch-climbers, pickpockets, halfwits,
jewel thieves, professional maimers, yeggmen, ex-
convicts and, in its later days, adepts at kidnaping or
the "snatch racket."

Certainly the night club, at its worst and most
flamboyant, had a direct connection with crime. It
had its very origin in disrespect for the prohibition

law.   Instantly it appealed to the criminal as a source
of business.

The record is pretty.   The Club Chantee, destroyed
by fire in 1926, was operated by Richard Reese Whittemore and his gang of thieves and murderers.   Whittemore, who was hanged for murder in Baltimore,
had with him, either as waiters or other employees
at the club, such thieves as the redoubtable "Shuffles"
Goldberg and Anthony Paladino, and the two Kraemer
boys, Jake and Leon, recognized in the underworld
as the greatest safe crackers in history.   Some of the
gang are dead now, and others are in jail, but while
they had the Chantee it was a grand place for a man
to take his wife or his sweetheart.

Owen Madden, who had got out of Sing Sing in
1923, had an interest in many clubs—no one ever was
able to figure out how many.   Madden, however, for
all his record, was regarded as being far above such
low harpies as the Whittemore gang.   Madden's
friend and sometime partner, Bill Duffy, also with a
record, ran the Silver Slipper for a time, and his last
known eating and drinking venture before he decided
to devote all his time to making a heavyweight
champion out of Primo Carnera was Duffy's Tavern,
in West Forty-fourth Street, where Keen's Chop
House once delighted the judicious with its steaks,
chops and chutney.   "Big Frenchy" DeMange, who
had a criminal record, also ran a night club.

There were others: Charles Fern, with a record a yard long, mostly for picking pockets, ran the Ferndale and later a speakeasy just off lower Fifth Avenue, where, when a policeman was killed while interfering with a robbery, Fern was forced to say farewell to business in New York; James Redmond, no better than he should have been, who ran the Parody; Red Sheehan, tough and terrible, who ran the Rendezvous before he was sent to Sing Sing; Benny Mohr, alias Moore, who had a club in East Fifty-fourth Street and was a pal of the notorious "Skush" Thomas, whose bad manners caused another gangster to knock his brains out with a baseball bat in Atlantic City.

Nice boys. And yet, though it may seem strange to an outlander, some of them served good liquor, good food, fair entertainment and kept a close eye on their joints to prevent crime—at any rate, crime of a too flagrant nature. The clubs, however, were essentially business enterprises, and it was next to impossible to keep away the criminal taint. Instead of being founded solidly on reputations for sound, inexpensive eating, the clubs often rented out to different men the kitchen, soft drink, cloakroom, cigarette and taxicab concessions. The system left itself wide open for crookedness and trouble.

The petty rackets grew—raising the bill, raising checks, trying out genteel blackmail on men with women other than their wives, adding empties to the list of drinks consumed and what not. There also was the popular hostess racket, by which the hostess sipped drinks made of colored water which were charged to the sucker, who thought he was having a grand time talking to her and plying her with strong drink.

Although competition was murderous between the clubs, and the constant raidings made the business extremely hazardous, the gay life continued through the years. Every now and then a prophet would announce that the night club was dead, that there were no more free spenders, that the radio was keeping people at home; but such prophets were wrong. The profits were too large to give up.

Some of the ordinary prices: $1 for ten Camel cigarettes in a special package; $6 for a rag doll; $4.50 for four roses as a boutonnière; $1 for a paper gardenia; $2 for a pitcher of water; $10 for a pint of whisky and $1 for a small bottle of White Rock. On the last night of 1928 cover charges in Texas Guinan's new Club Intime ranged from $20 upward. At the Montmartre the charge was $20, at the Lido $15, at the Heigh-ho $15, and so on all through the list— and this after a year in which the Federal Government, as well as the New York City police, had been more than usually active in harassing the night places.

Mayor James J. Walker, who was no prude but who was hardly what might be called a habitué of

night clubs, was worried about the occasional murders, beatings and fights which occurred in the clubs,
not to mention the occasional complaints of check
raising. He said he had good reason to believe that
many clubs were hangouts for "white collar thieves."
Moreover, it gave a bad impression to the poor working man, on his way to honest labor at dawn, to see
groups of tipsy people in evening clothes coming out
of night clubs. That way lay Bolshevism. Walker
believed a three o'clock curfew would be sensible, and
such an ordinance was passed. It didn't do much
good.

Later, Police Commissioner Edward P. Mulrooney
expressed the opinion that a one o'clock curfew was
needed. Some of the Harlem places, whither pleas-
ure-seekers had been flocking in numbers since Florence Mills's singing and Carl Van Vechten's writings
had helped make New York color-conscious, objected
to the early curfew, and so did many of the Broadway places, which pointed out that they depended
on the after-theater trade. Finally, after months of
argument, the police got the right to regulate the
clubs.

Mr. Mulrooney summoned the night club and
dance hall proprietors to Police Headquarters and
gave them a good talking to. There should be no
more closed dance halls, with paid girls to dance with
men; no more subsidized taxicabs to bring in drunks

to be rolled; no more gangsters, thugs or racketeers were to be let into clubs; and no more licenses to be granted to establishments in small rooms. The police got busy checking the clubs and their employees, dividing the good from the bad. It is probable that this system, which generally was under the administration of an honest but reasonable set of police officials, has proved about the most effective in keeping to a minimum the more objectionable features of the night clubs. Even so, it is far from perfect; no scheme ever will be so long as people have money and insist on having an exciting place in which to spend it.

What really changed the night clubs after the period of their rankest growth was the stock market collapse of 1929. It was many months before the effects were noticed, but by the summer of 1933 the clubs had been thinned to a point where only the healthiest could survive. It is doubtful if New York, for many a day, will ever support, at one time, the seventy or more profitable centers of night life which flourished in the days when the sky was the limit. Night life definitely turned toward the home, the hotel grills and roofs, the inexpensive places in Greenwich Village, a few Harlem resorts, and the beer gardens and roadhouses in the suburbs.

The amount of money involved in the organization of the clubs may be guessed at from information contained in a memorandum which came into the possession of a newspaper in 1931, but which never was printed. A syndicate of bootleggers, actually headed by a small group of New York's best known racketeers, was dickering with Joseph Urban for the decoration of a luxurious establishment in the East Fifties. It seems that these mugs, who didn't know anything about art, but who knew what they liked when they saw it, had taken a peek at Urban's work in the Central Park Casino and decided that it was just the sort of thing they wanted.

Urban was an architect at heart and took such jobs only with considerable reluctance. He asked $50,000 and got it—$15,000 in cash and the rest in notes. The new place, according to information disclosed in the memorandum, was one of a chain of twenty-three similar places, all owned and operated by the same group. What struck the man who wrote the memorandum as amusing was not the great amount of money which must have been tied up in the organization, but the dreadful time the head gangsters, who were far from erudite men, were having in getting through their heads the meaning of such complicated processes as amortization, second mortgage foreclosures and other financial permutations. Those things simply can't be reduced to words of one syllable.

New York was hospitable, and still is, to some of the strangest types of *entrepreneur* who ever tried to run a place of entertainment, but the city also has wrecked the hopes of others. Usually a nod from the police means the end of the dreams of a night club operator, who might as well fade away.

Others over-capitalize and guess wrong on what will attract customers. Joe Zelli came over from Paris and opened the Royal Box; he lost virtually all except his shirt, and sailed back for France broke but philosophical. Texas Guinan, who had to put up with the almost incessant harrying of the police, found Chicago more profitable.

Their adventures, however, were mild compared to what happened to poor old Belle Livingstone. Back in the nineties this fabulous person used to be toasted as "the chorus girl with the poetic legs." She had been a deserted child, she said, and had been found under a sunflower in Kansas by John Ramsay Graham, founder of the Emporia *Gazette*. Mr. Graham adopted her. Later she married actors, millionaires and other men, and finally, in the autumn of her life, came back to New York and announced that she was going to open in Park Avenue "a salon of culture, wit and bonhomie." It was all of that for a time, and then she was raided. In her defense she denied the sale of liquor, saying it was all a sort of complicated Dutch treat arrangement.

Stubborn, she opened a place in East Fifty-eighth Street, with a fine bar and grillroom, a riot of decoration, with equipment for miniature golf and ping-

pong. The resort occupied five floors. Again she was
raided. What of it? She kept right on and then
was raided again while four hundred guests were in
her "country club." She tried to escape over the
rooftops, but Andrew McCampbell's alert prohibition agents recognized her by her red pajamas and
caught her.

When she came into court she said she didn't own
the "country club" (she was telling the truth), but
she wouldn't divulge who did. She was found guilty
of violating a personal injunction against selling
liquor and was sent to prison for thirty days. She
had a sort of coming-out party when her term was up.
She had lost ten pounds and appeared happy. Texas
Guinan sent an armored car to escort her back to
Broadway. Her morals, she said, had not been im-
paired by contact with the other prisoners; on the
contrary they had, if anything, been improved. A
month later she was enjoined from violating the prohibition law in the Southern District of New York;
then she went bankrupt for more than $30,000. That
was the end of Mme. Livingstone in New York City.
She went West, and in the summer of 1933 was back
in the East, running a resort at West Hampton, near
the eastern end of Long Island. Footnote on prohibition: The building where she operated her "country
club" was still operating, after many raids by both
police and Federals, in the summer of 1933. It was

called the Park Avenue Club, with decorations by
Joseph Urban, and it was one of the most popular,
and best, clubs in the city.

Not all the places of New York's effulgent era were
revolting to decency, and not all of them were dull.
Moreover, they gave a chance to many entertainers of
great talent, some of whom, starting with no reputation at all, became famous and wealthy. A cross-
section of the people and the places:

El Garron, when Georges Fontana and Anna Lud-
milla were there.

The Mayfair Yacht Club, below the level of the
street, with the waters of the East River, pretty at
night, flowing by.

The Bath Club, when John Perrona ran it.

Ciro's, with Clifton Webb and Mary Hay giving
humorous dancings.

The Trocadero, with Emil Coleman's music and
Fred and Adele Astaire dancing. Leonora Hughes
and Maurice used to be there.

The Lido, with Edythe Baker and Billy Reardon,
who later became Barbara Bennett's partner.

The Club Alabam', with an agile brownskin show
and Johnny Hudgins, in the days when the African
trend was going strong, together with such places
as the Bamville, the Cotton Club, the Nest, and
Gladys's Exclusive Club, where the songs were, to be
blunt about it, filthy.

The Club Durant, named for Jimmy Durante of the long nose, whose humor, if that's what it was, was so violent and insane that even years later it was difficult to understand.

The Club Richman, before Harry Richman went on to greater fame, and its practically naked dancing.

The Back Stage Club, where Frisco was master of ceremonies.

The Texas Guinan Club, where one of her girls, Ruby Keeler, who later married Al Jolson, sang with a lisp.

The Crillon, in the old place in Forty-eighth Street, where Otto Baumgarten served excellent food and where the murals by Winold Reiss were good to look at.

Riley's Arrowhead Inn, where the music was fair, the frogs' legs splendid and some of the people not so charming.

The Beaux Arts Restaurant, on the eighth floor, with Fay Marbe as entertainment.

The very swank Embassy Club, where, one night, Mrs. Richard T. Wilson, president of the club, asked a waiter to pursue a girl who was shedding glass beads and to mop them up with brushes.

The hot summer of 1925, when Texas Guinan ran her place at Valley Stream, Long Island, and the night when there was a great lot of noise because James J. Walker, who was running for Mayor, dropped in.

Sometimes Texas, to be cute, wore a necklace of pad-locks.

The Owl Club, which had four booths housing chefs of four nationalities—Mexican, Chinese, Italian and Negro—and where the waiters would put on a show without any reason.

Barney's, down in the old place in Third Street, where things were restful, well-bred, with celebrities walking about.

Don Dickerman's many places in the Village—the County Fair, the Blue Horse, the Pirate's Den, etc. Dickerman, who served as a scientist on one of William Beebe's expeditions, won a prize in 1931 for a definition of love ("A season pass on the shuttle between heaven and hell"), and then went bankrupt in 1932.

The Montmartre, when the remarkably suave Charlie Journal, whose knowledge of night life is the most nearly perfect of them all, was in command.

The doings of Roger Wolfe Kahn, son of the banker Otto, who lost a lot of money on his night club, Le Perroquet.

Small's, in Harlem, where the waiters did the Charleston, late at night, while carrying fully loaded trays.

The Mirador, when the Fokine ballet was there.

The Greenwich Village Inn, with out-of-town people and Villagers strangely mixed, all panting for excitement.

The Lido-Venice when Captain Guardabassi ran it. It was so snooty that it had to give way to a reorganization to make people feel at home.

The Forty-fifth Street Yacht Club, in the nights when Tommy Lyman was bringing it to life.

The strange place in Forty-sixth Street, in the basement, called the Cave of the Fallen Angels.

Helen Morgan singing her throaty songs, sitting on top of a piano, in her Fifty-fourth Street place.

The sage advice of Bernarr Macfadden's *Graphic*, which had an etiquette column telling working girls how to behave. One admonition: "Empty your mouth before kissing in public places."

The new Little Club, when Phil Baker, Sid Silvers and Marian Harris were the attractions.

Felix, the headwaiter with the pointed nose, down at Mori's in Bleecker Street.

The unfortunate interval when Evelyn Nesbit came back to town and opened a night club. One night Harry K. Thaw came in, didn't like the check he got, and threw the dishes on the floor. Always petulant.

The Jungle Room, rough, noisy and primitive.

The days when the knowing were fooled by the Club Chantee, before they knew it was run by the

Whittemore mob. They thought it was high class because it was hard to get in.

The coming of the great Rudy Vallee to the Heigh-ho.

The girl at Texas Guinan's who did a dance with a sleepy eight-foot boa constrictor.

The Casanova, when it had Morton Downey and Helen Kane.

The Midnight Frolic, with its $6.60 cover charge and Paul Whiteman.

The coming of Duke Ellington to the Cotton Club out in Harlem, and the rush of white people to the place.

Libby Holman, the blues singer, at the Lido in 1929, before her marriage and the death of her husband, Smith Reynolds.

The Club Abbey, of sour memory. It was loud and nasty, with the "cuff corner," or free pews, always occupied by sinister characters. One night there was a whale of a fight there, with gun-play, and the club was no more.

The Drool Inn, of all names, in Harlem, where the fun was excruciatingly low-down.

The swanky Sutton Club, with Douglas Byng and Beatrice Lillie.

George Olsen and his orchestra, and his theory that the tomtom is the basis of all dance music.

The perennial argument among the experts over

whether Harry Richman really coined the phrases
"butter-and-egg man," "Hello, sucker!" and "Give
the little girl a great big hand."

Maurice Mouvet, the sickly, temperamental, much-
married dancer, who had a hard time making people
believe he was born in New York.

The Hollywood, with the droves and droves of
good-looking girls and with Nils T. Granlund as
master of ceremonies.

The virtuous denial of the engaging Hyman
(Feets) Edson that his place sold liquor. "We're
honest," he said. "We get $6 from everybody who
sits down and $1.50 for a glass of ginger ale. We
don't have to sell liquor."

The closing of La Vie because Frank Wallace had
been found murdered at its door.

Some curious names of joints: The Furnace, the
Hyena Club, the Ha! Ha!, the Day Breakers, the Jail
Club, the Eugenic Club.

The loud laughter which went up when Joab H.
Banton, District Attorney of New York County,
made the cautious announcement that he had discovered that a gunman was reputed to have an interest in a club.

The exploits of Walter Longcope, the prohibition
agent with the society manners, who conducted the
most famous raid on Texas Guinan's place. He later

married Mrs. Jesse Livermore, divorced wife of the Wall Street speculator.

The great reform of 1928, when the ribald life underwent a change to please the police. The girls, instead of being allowed to mix with the guests and create all manner of confusion, were told to go to their rooms between shows, where they could sew, smoke, read the *Daily Mirror* or talk to one another without bothering the customers.

The great luck of Tommy Guinan, brother of Texas, who, although raided and arrested many times, never got into any serious trouble.

These people, and these places, filled a need which, however silly and anti-social it might have been at bottom, seemed real enough at the time. The night clubs—most of them certainly—will be replaced by something else, depending largely upon the regulations which are adopted by New York for the regulation of the sale of hard liquor and real wine.

While they lasted the clubs contributed more than anything else to the madhouse that was New York. If some of the night club owners were pretty bad, some of the customers were worse. They would kick about the bill, when they had expected to be robbed in the first place; they would try to drink up the town's booze supply in one night; they would drink too much and then try to lead the band; they would lose their rolls and then blame the wrong people for it; they would get reeling, blind drunk and try to steal their neighbors' girls; they would tip so much that they were ridiculous or so little that they would be snubbed; they would raise a terrible ruckus in a futile attempt to get ringside seats at a place that already was full; they had, some of them, no more sense than to listen to the siren call of a taxi-cab driver who said, "Want to meet some nice girls, buddy?" In short, the lower stratum of customers were obstreperous, ill-mannered, unable to hold their liquor, and ripe for the plucking.

The wonder of it is that there were not more killings, beatings, stabbings and robberies. The life and property of most drunks appears to be protected by Providence; surely the police can't protect them all. The invasion by the whites of the Harlem clubs, in particular, created a situation which could have caused serious trouble. It didn't; only in a few instances was trouble reported, and then it usually was in a very cheap place where a white man had no business going.

The vogue of the female impersonator in the clubs (there was even a place called the Club Pansy) might also have caused more trouble than it did. As it was, this era caused little except a faint nausea, and the police, with their traditional hatred of the intermediate sex, kept their nightsticks poised.

Of the whole period, the most poignant and re-vealing story is of the rich young man, far gone in liquor, who one night entered a night club and found himself, while seeking the washroom, in a small room which seemed, even in his befuddled state, vaguely familiar. The pictures on the wall came back to him. Then he knew that this house had been the place where he had lived as a little boy, and this room had been his nursery. He got his hat and went out into the clean air.

OWNEY, THE OLD MASTER

OWEN VICTOR MADDEN, once the leader of the old Gopher (pronounced "Goofer") gang back in the innocent days before the war, gained a reputation as a youth for being very tough indeed. He was born in Liverpool in June, 1892, and came to New York at the age of eleven. Now, of all the tough Micks which are spawned from Nome to Cape Town, a Liverpool Mick is held by experts to be the toughest of them all. He was at home in the Hell's Kitchen section of New York, where, with a record of forty-four arrests, sometimes for homicide, he earned the sinister title of Owney the Killer—a title which he always detested.

He was sent to Sing Sing in 1915 upon his conviction of having instigated a killing. He was paroled in 1923 and came back to the city. A lesser man, a man of more limited imagination, or one who had been broken by prison, would have slipped back into the underworld as a mere punk, a nobody. Madden had iron in his gizzard. He found a changed city, a city of night clubs and speakeasies and rackets. He became, in many respects, the most important man in New York. He also was one of the most misunderstood. They called him all sorts of things, but it is

true that among his friends he was held in high esteem
—and some of these friends were honest cops who had
grown up with him on the West Side. Hell's Kitchen
is the nursery for some of the finest policemen and
some of the most ruthless criminals. Take your pick.

Madden became the Elder Statesman, the Grand
Old Man, of the rackets of New York. His word,
except among madmen and low competitors who had
designs upon his life or his money, was always, in the
days of his glory, regarded as absolutely good. This
man, whose long-ago record caused him to be referred
to occasionally as a sneak-thief and worse, actually
had a great many admirable qualities. It would have
been impossible for even the most strict moralist to
have passed an afternoon listening to Owney without
feeling that, according to his own lights, he was an
honest man.

He was shaped into a master by the crusades of
Wayne B. Wheeler, Mrs. Ella A. Boole, Bishop James
Cannon, Jr., and all the rest of that steadfast band
who gave prohibition to a bewildered nation. The
reformers created out of the old New York a gaudy,
upside-down metropolis of the sort which Madden
was born to rule. And the little jailbird came back
to thrive on the lush, green pastures of Manhattan.
He had been cast down; the prohibitionists, unconscious of what they were doing, gave him a reason for
being. The civilization that they had created wel-

comed him back, a frail and almost forgotten figure
of legend, and made him master.

In the summer of 1930 a lawyer who had handled
many of his business affairs said that, although it
would be impossible to estimate with any degree of
accuracy the total wealth of Madden, it would surely
amount to more than a million dollars.

Millionaires and their ladies drank the Madden
booze in many a joint. Gentlemen of the fancy sat
at the ringside of Madison Square Garden and watched
pugilists controlled by Madden. Other people sent
their linen to Madden's laundry.

He was, in the period when his power was great,
one of the most genuine of all the big post-war
racketeers. It is strange, too, that he looked the part
—not like the coarse, beefy, jolly Al Capone, but like
the lean, hard and catlike gentlemen who act such
parts on the stage. His appearance has been described
many times, usually by persons who never saw him,
and there has persisted a curious fiction that the expression on his face was innocent, that he might, indeed, be called "cherubic" or "baby-faced." Nothing
could be more arrant moonshine. He looked and
acted precisely as a racketeer should look and act.

If a theatrical manager had put Owney on the
stage, to act the part of Owney Madden, the critics
would have said that it was just a little too perfect for
honest realism. But it would have been the most

natural thing in the world, speech, mannerisms and clothes. It sounds shocking to those who have admired Madden from a great distance, but he actually said "dese," "dem" and "dose." And all his life he was addicted to saying "youse." These expressions in no wise interfered with his progress; he wasn't interested in joining the Racquet and Tennis Club anyhow. To his friends his lapses in pronunciation were easily forgiven; to others, particularly ladies who had heard of him and were thrilled at meeting him for the first time, these lamentable faults served only to enhance his charm. To some he appeared "cute."

His face was small. In profile its lines were like a falcon's. His forehead was not high, and it receded a little. The nose was a fierce beak. He had that first requisite of leadership, "a bone in the face." His mouth and chin dropped away almost straight to the neck. No offense meant, but, when viewed from the front, there was something fishlike about the way the mouth drooped at the corners. His face was sometimes pallid and sometimes flushed. His body bore the scars of many bullets, and the condition of his lungs always made him fear that he would die of tuberculosis. His hair was black and sleek. His eyes were blue, a very bright and piercing blue. Sometimes they were friendly enough, and in repose they were even sad, but usually they were hard, and shining, and they saw everything.

Back in the Gopher days an exasperated police sergeant called him "that little banty rooster out of
hell," and he always had about him some of that alert
and truculent cockiness.

In many ways he had more sense than Capone. He
was a better business man. He saw what too much
publicity was doing for Capone. Already shy of the
limelight, he became frantic when he saw references
to him, or to his old record, in print. There are many
pictures of Capone available for anyone who wants to
reproduce them—Capone smiling, Capone fishing,
Capone in meditation, and what not. But, up until
the early part of 1932, when he was picked up as a
parole violator and sent back to Sing Sing, there were
only two pictures of Madden available. One was a
profile view taken during the trial for the killing
which sent him to prison, and the other was the regulation front view Rogues' Gallery masterpiece, taken
at about the same time, and showing his shirt collar
open at the front. It was, to him, a sure sign of doom
when a racketeer began getting too much publicity.
All publicity, to Owney, was bad publicity.

He was, in his way, a good deal of a salty wisecracker, a master of shockingly picturesque figures of
speech. When he was being very positive about something, he would say that he would "bet all the tea in
China" that he was right. When steamed up, he could
tell an amazingly graphic story. He liked to rise from

his seat and act out the more vivid parts. Sometimes
these stories were appalling in their cruelty. Once,
without mentioning real names, he acted out the saga
of what he said was the only man who had been taken
for a ride in New York and who came back alive.
Owney started at one end of the room, with a description of how the man had been put into an automobile.
Then came the blow over the head, the taping of the
mouth, the gentle ministrations of the killers, who
didn't want him to die until they got him out in the
country. Then came the great scene, with the victim
blindfolded, backed up against a tree, and his fingers
stuck in the barrels of a shotgun. Owney's delinea-
tion of the anguish of the victim, and the cold horror
of the scene, were as good as anything ever put into
a gang play or a gang picture. His gestures could be
deliberate, but usually his hands were quick and electric, and his body gave the impression of great tense-
ness.

He was articulate, and some of his aphorisms were
of more than ordinary penetration. For a long time
he was disgusted with his laundry. He had sunk a lot
of money in it, perhaps more than a quarter of a
million dollars. Not only did it fail to make money,
but it was a constant worry.

"I'd like to get out of it," he said. "I like an in-
vestment where you can put your money in this week
and pull it out double next week, or the next. But

these legitimate rackets—" (his eyes blazed with murderous fury at the thought)—"you've got to wait for your money."

There was enunciated the guiding economic principle of Madden—and of all the other racketeers on earth. For the most part he took care that his rackets were sensible: that is, they entailed no long wait for the pay-off.

It is doubtful if any one man, even among his close friends and partners, such as William V. ("Big Bill") Dwyer, William Duffy, George DeMange ("Big Frenchy"), Gustave Guillame ("Little Frenchy") and Jerry Sullivan, could have given a list of all the enterprises in which Madden had an interest of one sort or another. And of course he was suspected of being interested in a great many projects of which he had never heard. People sometimes used his name to intimidate people who had no reason to feel afraid.

At one time Madden was supposed to have control of the Cotton Club in Harlem, one of the most popular centers of night life in the black belt. Again he was said to have controlled the Silver Slipper, and again it was said on Broadway that he controlled one of Texas Guinan's resorts. There were other stories —stories that he supplied the liquor to hundreds of night clubs and speakeasies, and that he was so close to the management that he was even consulted on decorations.

Once the Cotton Club had a rival. The Plantation opened in Harlem, catering to about the same sort of clientele as the Cotton. One night a wrecking crew came down upon the Plantation. They left the place a shambles; the joint wasn't worth ten cents when they had finished. The police thought they saw evidences of the old-time Madden brass-knuckle technique, but they couldn't begin to prove anything, and nothing was ever done about it.

A few months later Harry Block, who was one of Madden's partners in the Cotton Club, was shot and killed. Nobody cared much, but some people said that the murder was in retaliation for the ruin of the Plantation. There was no evidence.

If it is true, as alleged, that Owney had obtained a percentage of the booze racket in Harlem, in addition to his interests in the mid-town section, his profits must have been enormous. He was commonly supposed to be the real management, with Dwyer, of the brewery of the Phœnix Cereal Beverage Company in West Twenty-sixth Street, where "Madden's No. 1," a fine brew, was made. Time and again the Federal people tried to close the brewery, but, except for a few temporary victories, they might as well have left it alone.

Madden had a good eye for a promising pugilist. He usually sat a few rows back from the ring at Madison Square Garden, with a small group of his

friends, and he surveyed the doings inside the ring
with the eye of a connoisseur. With Bill Duffy and
Big Frenchy he owned most, or all, of Primo Carnera,
the giant Italian prizefighter who came over in 1930
and toured the country knocking out set-ups.

And yet, for all his strong position, his interlocking
directorates, and his firm grip upon his lieutenants,
he was extremely nervous. Without seeking it, he
began to receive too much publicity. It became the
convenient thing to refer to him as the chief racketeer
of New York, and to compare him with Chicago's
Capone. He was becoming a symbol, and he couldn't
prevent it. He knew that, no matter how careful a
man might be, he could still be taken for a ride. He
knew the danger of the paid assassin. He knew, too,
that among the army of thugs in New York, there
were a few who would have shot him just to get the
reputation of being very dangerous. One night a
whisper went along that Vincent Coll, the stupid,
reckless killer who was later rubbed out by machine-
gun fire while telephoning from a drugstore not far
from Madden's home, had planned to kidnap John
Marrin, Madden's brother-in-law. Again, the story
went around that Coll planned the ultimate in daring,
the kidnaping of Owney himself. This story probably is true, for Coll was crazy enough for such an
adventure. Certainly Coll "put the snatch" on
Owney's partner, Big Frenchy, one night, took him

to a house in White Plains and refused to release him until Madden had raised $20,000, which Madden paid.

He was afraid also of being framed, either by the police or by enemies in the underworld. He knew a great many policemen, and it implies nothing discreditable to anyone to say that he was on good terms with many of them. He was glad always to run as fast as he could to Police Headquarters when he was wanted for anything. If possible, he liked to be accompanied by veteran detectives who he knew would not doublecross him for whatever fleeting fame there might be in it. "No strange cop is ever going to arrest me," he said once. There was sense back of that decision; he knew how easy it was for gunmen to pose as policemen, force a man into an automobile and take him for the last journey on earth.

Fakers and liars annoyed him. Many a time a silk burglar, or a jewel robber, would tell the police that Owney had hired them to do the job, which would throw Madden into a horrible rage. He was forced to submit to all manner of petty shake-downs; his largesse, merely to appease the army of harpies who thought he had all the money in the world, was tremendous. It wasn't the most comfortable life in the world.

With all its shortcomings, however, the New York that Madden found when he got out of Sing Sing in 1923 was just about as well suited for his purposes as if he had created it all himself, for himself. Up in prison he had been listening to tales of the new crop of rackets, with alcohol as their base. Much of it sounded fantastic. But what he saw upon his return to Broadway made his blue eyes gleam. Back in Hell's Kitchen a "racket" meant a benefit dance. Now it meant big business, everything from the little neighborhood shopkeepers' associations to the really big rackets like the now defunct Bank of United States.

Owney got busy. This was home, but how different! The underworld was growing smooth, well-dressed and polite. The days were gone when gangs fought each other for sheer love of battle, or for some trivial point of honor or prestige. It was silly to think of breaking into box-cars and little drygoods-stores, as the Gophers of sweet memory had done. It was a day of mergers, combines, large-scale organization.

Madden first lent his services to a taxicab company as a sort of consultant on industrial relations: that is, his job was to protect the company from unfair competition, which in turn means to muscle the opposition out of the field. This job lasted only a few months, long enough for a breathing spell while he got his bearings.

He had been out of prison almost a year when a strange occurrence was reported. The telephone rang at the Liberty Storage Warehouse in West Sixty-fourth Street.   James Stafford, the seventy-one-year-old watchman, answered it.

"This is Mr. Woods," said a voice. "I left a package at the office and I'm sending my secretary over for it. Please let him in."

The old man thought he recognized the voice of Woods, one of the owners of the warehouse. The package was described in detail. In a few minutes there was a knock on the door, and a well-dressed man who said he was Mr. Woods's secretary stood there, asking for the package. Stafford tried to find the package, but couldn't, and suggested that the man hunt for it himself. The "secretary" entered, followed the watchman to the door of the office, and then seized him from behind. Three other men came through the opened door. They bound and gagged the old man and carried him to the second floor, where they placed him on a mat. Soon he heard the rumble of a truck leaving the building. That truck contained 200 cases of bonded rye whisky valued at $16,000.

Four detectives learned that the stolen truck had broken down not far from the warehouse and had been towed away by another truck, with a Cadillac sedan following closely behind. The stolen truck was found empty the next day in West Forty-fourth Street. The detectives watched it for two hours. Three men came up to the truck and started to open

its doors. There was no fight. At the police station
they said they were Owen Madden, Harry Jacobs and
George DeMange (Big Frenchy). They were held
in $10,000 bail each for assault and robbery, but noth-
ing was ever done about it. There was not much
evidence. It all looked queer; that was all.

Then in January, 1924, state troopers arrested six
men riding on a truck loaded with $25,000 worth of
liquor in Westchester County. The liquor had been
stolen from the home of Charles Mayer, a broker, at
Stockbridge, Mass. One of the prisoners gave the
name of James Malloy, but the police found that he
was Owney Madden. Owney explained that he had
been hitch-hiking and had begged for a ride on the
truck. It was as much of a shock to him as to anyone else, he said, to learn that it was a truck full of
stolen booze. Nothing was ever done about this,
either.

In the following April Joab H. Banton, then District Attorney of New York County, wrote a letter
to James L. Long, State Superintendent of Prisons,
urging that Owney be returned to Sing Sing to serve
out the rest of his term, which was from ten to twenty
years. It was just another letter. Nothing was done.
Banton pointed out that twice in a year Madden had
been arrested in company with men of long records
for criminal violence, and under the law he could be

returned to prison merely for associating with such people.

One night a Broadway detective, who had known Madden for many years, saw him in the company of a woman who had a jail record. "I suppose I ought to pick you up and send you up the river again," said the detective, "but I'm not going to. Listen, you'd better watch your step."

All these things made Madden think. Not until 1932, when he was sent back to prison, did he ever have any serious trouble with the law. Only two arrests! In his journeyman days, back with the Gophers, he had been arrested forty-four times. Now he began to acquire subtlety. He became a master technician. In his own mind, as he became more sure of himself, his enterprises took on a respectable quality. He became a sort of philosopher.

"What's the matter with rackets?" he once asked in one of his frequent disquisitions to friends. "They're a real benefit to the small tradesman. Take the laundry racket, for instance. Why, I'll bet all the tea in China that half the little guys in the business would be starving to death if it wasn't for the racket. They get protection, don't they, from independents? If some mug opens a laundry where he ain't wanted, the boys tell him to scram the hell out of the neighborhood, don't they? The racket's a genuine benefit in cases like that."

More respectable thinkers than Owney, men with important names in industry, have put the same idea into different words. It is simply the argument for getting rid of unfair or ruinous competition.

When he was in a mellow mood (he rarely ever drank much, but he could unbend) he liked to talk of the old days when he and his wild hellions ravaged the West Side from Forty-second to Fourteenth streets. In retrospect these lads would appear not as bruisers, loft thieves, pickpockets and what not, but as good-hearted lads full of the spirit of fun and horseplay. "Wildest bunch of roosters you ever saw," is how he remembered them.

He always protested that he was innocent of the charge of causing the murder of William Moore, alias Little Patsy Doyle. Moore, remembered on the West Side as "a husky guy with two gold teeth," met his doom on November 28, 1914, in a saloon at Eighth avenue and Forty-first street.

"I didn't have it done," he would say, "but I have no kick coming. I believe in the law of compensation. All those times I was arrested, in all those years, the cops had me right, but I lied my way out of it. They never had enough evidence. Then they got me for something I didn't do, and wouldn't believe me when I told the truth. But that's all right. I'm not sore at the state, or anybody. I've paid my debt. That's all wiped out now."

Madden always insisted that the slate had been wiped clean. He had served his time. He and society were even. And he regarded it as exceedingly bad taste for anyone to bring up his old record. Perhaps he was right. The old record has been told before, in different versions, but these outlines are correct:

It was Election Night, November 6, 1912, a night when Owney and every plug-ugly in town was busy. There was, that night, a "racket," which in those days meant a dance. The dance was given by the Dave Hyson Association in the Arbor Dance Hall at Seventh avenue and Fifty-second street. Hyson was a waiter. The dance was given in his name merely to beat the excise laws and sell liquor after hours. Madden and his young wife had been quarreling, and he had finally walked out on her. She sent word to him that on Election Night she would go to the dance and turkey-trot, bunny-hug or grizzly-bear with anybody she pleased. She did just that.

Then, late that night, Madden came in. He told them all to go ahead with their fun, while he retired to the balcony. A girl came up and talked to him. When she left he turned around and saw that he was surrounded by Hudson Dusters, the traditional enemies of the Gophers. They were on three sides of him. He dared them to shoot. He went down with at least six bullets in him.

In the hospital, where they thought he would die,

he laughed at everybody, gave them no information, and lived. It was while he was getting on his feet that Little Patsy Doyle, with his whispering tongue and conniving ways, began plotting against Owney. He was said to have been annoyed, also, because a woman named Freda Horner had been lost by him to Owney.

Little Patsy gathered his group of malcontents, did some slugging, and prepared to take over the leadership. The two factions—Owney versus Little Patsy —fought each other with roorbacks, blackjacks, guns and stilettos. Patsy became lonesome. The story was that he was to be "put on the spot," although that wasn't the concise phrase then. The prosecution always contended that Madden told off two of his gunmen, Bieler and McArdle, to do the job. Margaret Everdeane, friend of Freda Horner, was alleged to have helped lure Little Patsy into a saloon at Eighth Avenue and Forty-first Street—a spot which, in the years of his glory, Madden could never pass without getting an attack of the fantods and cursing the fate which got him into such a mess.

Anyhow, it seems that Margaret, Freda, and a gunpointer from the battleship *Brooklyn* named Willie the Sailor were sitting in the saloon. Margaret telephoned Little Patsy and told him Freda wanted to see him. Little Pasty came over and found Margaret and Willie (born William Mott) in the back room.

They told him Freda would be back soon. Patsy went to the bar. Bieler and McArdle tapped him on the shoulder. He whirled around. He was shot six times, and was on the floor once, but he had stamina enough to run out of the place. He fell dead in the hallway of a tenement. Bieler, McArdle and Madden were arrested three weeks later. The gunmen got long terms in Sing Sing, but Madden, the alleged instigator, who was under indictment for murder in the first degree, put up a bitter fight that lasted a week before he was convicted of manslaughter in the first degree. He had a tough time of it, for Willie the Sailor and Freda Horner and Margaret Everdeane all turned state's evidence and testified that Madden had remarked that he had wanted Little Patsy out of the way because he was "a squealer and a rat." They swore, moreover, that Madden had been lurking across the avenue while the shooting was going on, and that a few minutes later he appeared at a lunchroom a few blocks away and changed his cap and sweater for a hat and coat. Freda, the old darling, went even further, and told of Madden recounting to her later that night the whole details of the plot.

Whatever may have been the truth of all this, Judge Charles C. Nott in General Sessions, a tough judge, sentenced Madden to from ten to twenty years in Sing Sing. But Owney, even in those days, had friends. Subscription lists were started all over the

West Side to raise a defense fund to carry on his appeal. There were stories of intimidation for those who failed to subscribe. Then Freda and Margaret and Willie the Sailor recanted their testimony. The three were held for perjury, but nothing came of it.

Owney finally gave up and decided to serve his term without further battling. The day he made the decision was the day on which began his greatness. He set about, as all the really smart convicts do, to make himself a model prisoner. He never asked for special favors, even when he deserved them. He was a good influence among the other convicts, straightening out their foolish quarrels, arbitrating their petty differences, and making friends by the score.

Warden Lewis E. Lawes liked him. When the warden heard that an underworld celebrity was coming to join the prisoners, he would ask Owney his opinion of the expected guest. Owney would usually say the new man was "a smart fellow." One day, after a long procession of these "smart fellows" had received the Madden accolade, Warden Lawes pointed out that, taking the long view of things, perhaps they weren't such smart fellows after all—that all their smartness and all their striving had served only to bring them to Sing Sing. Madden, after pondering the warden's surmise, agreed that there might be something to that theory. Maybe they weren't smart.

Madden continued to be the model prisoner. He

was, even in the gray pile up the Hudson, still the
tough Liverpool Mick, the boss of the Gophers. He
was never an athlete. In 1920 the eight-year-old
wounds suffered from the guns of the Hudson Dusters began to bother him, and he underwent a major
operation. Again, in 1930, seven years after he had
been paroled from Sing Sing, the wounds bothered
him again, and he motored back to Sing Sing because
he would entrust himself to no one except Dr. Charles
Sweet, the prison surgeon. Then came pneumonia.
His tough fiber pulled him through.

It is not unusual for a man to form strong friend-
ships in prison. But Madden did more than that. It
is quite probable that he did more to set ex-convicts
on their feet, though he may have done it in curious
ways, than all the other social agencies put together.
That is why, in the years when he was a Big Shot, as
authentic a Big Shot as the underworld ever saw, he
was responsible for the employment of many men
who otherwise might have gone back to banditry.
During the period of his ascendency it would have
been possible to pass an evening having one's cab
driven by a Madden man, the door of the night club
opened by a Madden man, the food and drinks served
by a Madden man, and the clothes brushed by a Madden man back in the washroom. All of these may
have been ex-convicts, but they were under one strong
and terrible admonition from Owney: "Don't go

wrong. That is, don't get in trouble. Always be able to say you've got a respectable job."

Sometimes he would hear of a young man, a counterpart of one of the "roosters" of the old Gopher days, who was showing signs of acting up—robbing people, carrying a gun, talking too much and too loudly. He would either send word to the young man to behave himself or he would call the problem child before him and deliver a fierce, fatherly lecture on the blessings which come to the man who keeps out of trouble.

It was this perfectly sensible attitude which caused him to insist always upon outward order and decency in the conduct of the rackets of New York. He was suspicious of the swaggering tough boys from Chicago, Philadelphia and Boston. He saw no reason for killing anyone. There was, in those days, plenty of money for everybody. His hatred for the late Jack ("Legs") Diamond, the human sieve, may be traced to his realization that Diamond was a shallow thinker, too quick on the trigger, with a lust for blood and torture when there was no need for anything except a smile and an occasional firm command over the telephone. Madden could be firm. For all his nervousness, for all his dread of being framed or killed or betrayed, he would not back down in the face of minor racketeers who thought they could cow him.

He had his sentimental side, too. He loved his rela-

tives, his amusing pals, the little children of his partners and his neighbors, and above all he loved pigeons.
In his Gopher days he was a breeder of fancy pigeons.
He spent much money on them—Nun's Caps, Hol-
landers, Buda-Pesth Tiplitzes and other breeds. These
birds used to fly around New York, enticing birds
from other coops to come home with them, and many
fights ensued. Bieler, the gunman who killed Little
Patsy, said on the witness stand that it was unthink-
able that Owney would have hired him for the job,
as they were enemies. "We had a fight over some
boids," he explained, and he may have been telling
the truth. Owney, like all true pigeon fanciers, never
could understand how anyone could eat a pigeon.
The idea, somehow, smacked of cannibalism.

It was in the winter of 1931 that Madden, time
and again, was mentioned in connection with all manner of rackets. He was getting the publicity which
he had dreaded, and most of it was inaccurate. It was
discovered that he had been discharged from parole
years earlier by the Catholic Protective Society, into
whose hands he had been placed by the State Parole
Board. This meant that he did not have to report to
the board regularly, nor did he have to ask the board's
permission to make trips to Florida and California.
But, strangely, there was no record of this discharge,
and on January 23, 1932, the state board ordered
Madden to report regularly. Next came a hearing on

laundry rackets and one thing and another, and one Irving Levy, who described himself as president of the Hydrox Laundry in Brooklyn (Madden's old white elephant), testified that he had met Owney, but that Owney was not a stockholder and was not and never had been employed by the laundry. This contradicted Owney's testimony that he really was employed there, and the board promptly ordered Madden back to Sing Sing.

Owney won his first skirmish in the Supreme Court, but the state took an appeal, and on July 1 the Appellate Division reversed the Supreme Court Justice and decided that Owney must go back to Sing Sing. Owney, who had been out on bail pending appeal, was reported missing. Instantly the intrepid cops of Mexico, Canada and other places offered their services to search for the great racketeer. This hysteria didn't last long.

Late in the afternoon of July 6, 1932, a sedan drew up to the gates of Sing Sing. Owney got out. Two men drove away in the car. Owney walked up to the guard, a new man to whom the face of the great man meant nothing. The guard, puzzled by the spectacle of a man clamoring for entrance to Sing Sing, called another guard, and after a time Owney was admitted to his old home. They offered him supper, but he said he already had eaten. It was ruled a little later by the parole board that he must stay there for at least a year.

Madden was not well when he went to Sing Sing for the second time. At times he was enveloped in bitterness and melancholy. He was in the prison hospital for a time. Then he got better, helped clean the prison yard, tended the flowers and finally was placed in charge of the prison's flock of pigeons.

"I am glad to have him with me again," said Warden Lawes. "Not that I wish any man to be in prison, but he will help us here. He is a good influence upon the men."

There isn't any moral to any of this. What produced Madden? The slums of Liverpool? The slums of Hell's Kitchen and the tough roosters who slugged side by side with the old Gophers? The era of swanky night clubs and illicit booze? Out of Sing Sing, and with prohibition finished, he may become the boss of a respectable brewery, and settle down to a comfortable old age, with white horses to pull legitimate wagons piled with legitimate beer kegs across the streets of New York. Maybe so. He was a man who never knew his own strength. In his great days he could attend to the sinister business of parceling out the booze trade in the afternoon, and then drive down a little street crowded with children who, when they saw the familiar face peering out, would set up the friendly, hopeful chant: "Here's Uncle Owney! Here's Uncle Owney!"

A dreadful fellow, thoroughly anti-social. But the priests and the cops and the few close acquaintances who came to know him will all agree that, however twisted he may have become in the kickings he took from Liverpool to Sing Sing, he had in him a trace of genuine character. He came out of Sing Sing on parole on July 1, 1933, and went back into the shadows of New York.

THAT "DREADFUL" WINCHELL MAN

WALTER WINCHELL came to journalism pop-eyed with wonderment. He was, and still is, possessed of an almost maniacal curiosity. This astonishingly alert, electrically nervous little man has become, in the space of a few years, the most discussed, and in some respects the most important, newspaper man in New York. When he started his column on Bernarr Macfadden's old *Graphic* the wise men said he had invented a fad which couldn't possibly last more than two or three years; now his income is comparable to Arthur Brisbane's, and at breakfast his comments are read, by many, with the same eagerness with which others, tortured by the dreary afflictions of human society, reach for Walter Lippmann.

The secret of Winchell is that he is interested more in people than in ideas. As a newspaper formula this is far from new; indeed, it always has been the basis of the society "Personal" column and the jottings of the wool hat correspondent from Frog Hollow. Winchell applied the formula to New York, and more especially to that fabled, sinful street, Broadway.

Winchell did much for journalism, for which journalism has been slow to thank him. He helped to change the dreary, ponderous impersonality which was pervading the whole press. Do newspapers today print twice, or ten times, as many items about people—what they are like, what their crotchets are, what they eat and drink and wear—as they did ten years ago? Some of the credit belongs to Winchell. The man also fathered a crop of inferior tattlers.

There were other great columns, cut on a different pattern. The late Bert Leston Taylor, Franklin P. Adams, Don Marquis, Christopher Morley, H. I. Phillips—all these, with aphorisms, puns, poetry, urbane comment on the news and occasional philosophic disquisitions, were in the accepted tradition. It took Winchell to prove once more that people are interested in people and that facts, even trivial facts, have an irresistible fascination. Monastic fellows, most of the old line columnists, and for all their charm and erudition they weren't reporters. Winchell, put to the task of writing about Broadway, went out every night to see what Broadway was like.

This little man (he is a springy, smooth, good-looking chap, not yet forty, with prematurely gray hair) has been damned from the Battery to the Golden Gate. Men have boasted that if they ever saw him they would punch him in the snoot, but few ever did. His slang was denounced as vulgar, as corrupting the speech. He was called egotistical, and his doings were set down as being in very bad taste.

He has been accused of prying, of retailing low gossip, of printing information which might just as well have been kept hidden. To all this he seldom, if ever, made any defense.

His code, such as it is, is simple enough—he tries to get the news first, he protects his sources, and he never knowingly prints anything that might wreck a happily married home life. This last is to say that Winchell keeps quiet when he observes a married man or woman dallying with a person of the opposite sex in a night club, when he has reason to believe that the publication of such hot news might cause trouble at home.

Winchell writes of all sorts of people—bankers, politicians and playboys, but principally his news concerns the heroes and the villains of the theater, the motion picture, the radio and the night clubs. Few of these people resent invasions of what old-fashioned folks might call their privacy; even his announcements that a baby (or, as occurred in one instance at least, twins) was to be expected have seldom caused the persons involved more than temporary embarrassment. Indeed, it has been Winchell's experience that the majority are delighted to appear in his column.

He gets his news from a million sources. He accepts invitations to entertainments, and sometimes the host is so grateful to Winchell for coming that he tells Winchell a piece of news, worth only a paragraph to him, which in a few days will be all over the front pages. People buttonhole him on the street, waylay him in night clubs and restaurants, call him on the telephone frantically, to supply him with the stuff, some of it utterly inconsequential but interesting, which makes up his column.

Why do they do it? Not always because they are friends of his, though he is generally well liked on Broadway. Usually the motive is rooted in exhibitionism; the man who supplies Winchell with an item is warmed to his fingertips when he sees the item in print a day or two later. It makes him a member of the inner circle of gossips, a wise guy in the know, and increases his feeling of self-importance.

Will his vogue last? Of course it will—it or something very much like it—as long as there are people who are interested in the cruelties and kindnesses and follies of their neighbors.

Winchell brought to his job the perfect equipment —great energy, an eager desire to know what was going on, a lack of conventional breeding and experience, a mind delightfully free of book learning, and an unquenchable desire to be a newspaper man. If his background had been different, he would have been so befuddled by canons of what some people call good taste that he would have revolted at some of his best stuff. If he had been better educated (he never got beyond the sixth grade) he might have been dull.

As it was, everything he saw was news to him, a circumstance which accounts for his column, which runs about once a week, entitled "Things I Never Knew Till Now."

It was a gain for journalism that Winchell, when he started writing, didn't know the difference between "who" and "whom," a distinction which is not always clear even at this late day. He had been writing for years before he learned who Aristophanes was.

He was always stage-struck, and still is. He knew Eddie Cantor and George Jessel when they were children together. He quit school to be a singing usher in a motion picture house in Harlem, keeping crowds out of the aisles, collecting late checks and sometimes singing songs during intermissions. In 1910 he joined Gus Edwards's Newsboys' Sextette, traveling all over the country. Later he was manager of a company of eight, all older than himself, and then he had his own song and dance act with a partner. During the war he enlisted in the Navy and was for a time confidential secretary to an admiral.

After the war he went back into vaudeville. He was a fair song and dance man, but he had a terrific urge to be a newspaper man. He got out the *Daily News Sense,* consisting of several sheets of typewritten paper, which he would tack up beside the mailbox in every theater in which he appeared. It con-

tained intimate information about other actors on
the bill and personalities connected with the theater.
It became popular; managers liked it and local newspapers quoted from it. Occasionally he would send
a random column to *Billboard,* which was headed
"Stage Whispers." As far back as 1920 there appeared such items as these, in which the germ of the
later Winchell style may be clearly discerned:

"According to another trade paper, Mr. and Mrs.
Davey Jamison were blessed with a boy on January
23, at Portland, Me. On another page Mr. and Mrs.
J. were blessed with a boy January 25, at Portland,
Ore. Some leap. And whose airplane did the proud
parents use? Mother and child are doing fine. Con-
gratulations!"

"Most actors are married, and live scrappily ever
after."

"Did you ever notice the little brass tablet on the
door in the room of your hotel which reads: 'Stop!
Have you left anything?' Apropos of the H. C. of L.
it should read: 'Stop! Have you anything left?' "

"Seen outside of Cleveland movie theater: 'Geraldine Farrar supported for the first time by her husband.' "

"In New York recently the snow tied up traffic
severely. A gang hired to remove same struck at the
crucial moment, carrying banners which read: 'You
took away our beer, now take away the snow.' "

"A certain actress was left a fortune for being kind to a newspaper man. Moral: Be nice to column writers."

Glenn Condon, then editor of the *New York Vaudeville News*, saw some of Winchell's early stuff and liked it. Winchell had saved $1,500 from his $100-a-week salary as a hoofer, and he went to work for Condon at $25 a week for a trial period of six months. At the end of six months he was getting $50 a week; he was allowed 20 per cent on advertising, and soon his total income was greater than Condon's. Winchell credits Condon's tolerance and patience with being responsible for starting him on the way. In 1924 Fulton Oursler was organizing the *Graphic*, an afternoon tabloid, for Macfadden, and Winchell asked his friend, Norman Frescott, who knew Oursler, to speak for him, with the result that Winchell got the job as Broadway columnist.

For all his perky manner, Winchell during those first few months suffered from stage fright. He had never been a "regular" newspaper man, his paper was hardly what might be called a pillar of respectability and dignity, and he worked with a wild frenzy. He had gone to the *Graphic* for $100 a week, and four years later his salary was $300 a week. Then he went to the *Mirror*, a new morning tabloid. The *Graphic* soon died, and on the new paper Winchell became famous.

His contract with the *Mirror* calls for a flat salary of $1,000 a week. His profits from syndication of his column (papers all over the country take it despite the fact that it deals principally with people about whom few out-of-town readers have ever heard) vary from $250 to $400 a week. When busy, he is sure of at least $2,000 a week from the radio. He makes a motion picture short once a month for which he gets $3,500. The *Mirror* contract runs until October, 1935.

Winchell's headquarters are wherever he wants to make them. In New York he has an apartment at the Park Central Hotel. Sometimes he goes to Florida and Hollywood. He was in Miami Beach the night that Zangara attempted to kill President Franklin D. Roosevelt, and by luck, speed and ingenuity he was the first newspaper man to interview the assassin—a feat which caused Damon Runyon, the veteran reporter, to write a column in praise of Winchell, of which he is inordinately proud.

He stays up all night, and from sundown until dawn he may visit as many as a dozen places—theaters, restaurants, night clubs, private homes. He has been called bad names—scandalmonger, Little Boy Peep, the man at the keyhole, and the Peeping Tom of Journalism—but he is always a welcome guest and he probably has a more diverse acquaintance than any man in New York.

Wherever he goes there is an undercurrent of whispering. Diners in a restaurant may raise their heads here and there when a notable like Al Smith, Jack Dempsey, Primo Carnera or Jimmy Walker comes in, but the commotion aroused by the presence of these great men is a mere ripple compared with the sly pointings and head-noddings that fill the place when Winchell strides to his table. Does he like this attention? It is catnip, of course; vaudeville actors, as well as other people, crave attention even if they are doddering at the grave. Winchell's manner is that of the stage reporter.

The man has made a few mistakes. He has printed erroneous information, and many minor inaccuracies have crept into his accounts, but usually he is right, uncannily right. His informants seldom lie to him. One morning, or, rather, during the evening before when the newsboys were selling the first edition of the *Mirror*, there came a test of his accuracy. His column contained this statement:

"Five planes brought dozens of machine gats from Chicago Friday to combat The Town's Capone. . . . Local banditti have made one hotel a virtual arsenal and several hot-spots are ditto because Master Coll is giving them the headache. . . . One of the better Robin Hoods has a private phone in his cell! . . . Haw!"

Those who read the early papers thought that

sounded reasonable enough, although probably exaggerated, for it was well known that Coll, known as the Mad Dog, was in extremely bad odor with that faction of the underworld which frowned upon unnecessary violence. And Coll, a born killer and occasional kidnaper, had not been tamed.

At one o'clock that February morning Vincent Coll appeared from nowhere, walked into a drugstore in the Chelsea district and entered a telephone booth. He was having some difficulty with his call; indeed, it is said that, suspicious of the delay, he shouted to someone on the other end of the wire, "What the hell are you trying to do? Put me on the spot?" He didn't have much longer to wait. An automobile drew up to the curb and some men got out. One of them walked straight to the telephone booth and sprayed it, up and down and across, with machine-gun bullets. Coll toppled out, dead, and the killers went away from there.

The police, secretly, and most of the people of New York regarded the manner of the passing of Vincent Coll as natural and proper, and were not disposed to ask questions. But the District Attorney took Winchell before the Grand Jury, where the young man lost a lot of weight, but, apparently, he protected the source of his information, whatever that source might have been. There was talk of threats by letter and telephone for disclosing underworld secrets, and for a time Winchell went around with a bodyguard. The older, fundamentalist element among the racketeers believes, and with considerable good judgment, that it is bad policy for the plans of the gunmen and other feudists to be bandied about as if they were so many impending blessed events. Winchell always has had many good underworld sources of information; most of the mugs like him, they feel that they can trust his judgment on what not to print, and they admire him for making such an enormous success of what seems to them just another racket. And Winchell would rather be seen talking to a racketeer than to a bishop.

Many an aging newspaper reporter, who wanders about with dragging feet and drooping shoulders, possesses a wealth of just such information as Winchell has printed about the police, politicians and the underworld. The difference is that the ordinary reporter regards it as something to forget—certainly nothing to write about.

This brash historian of our life and times probably has deserved many a rebuke, but only once, so far as the records show, was he bawled out before a lot of nice people. That was on the night in January, 1932, when Winchell attended a party at the Central Park Casino given by A. C. Blumenthal, the theater owner and producer, and his wife, Miss Peggy Fears. A fair slice of the wit and beauty were there, and Win-

with the Shuberts. They barred him from their theaters because he consistently criticized their produc-
tions. Then Lee Shubert met Winchell's children in
Miami Beach, liked them, and said: "Well, I'm glad
to know there are some nice people in the Winchell
family." The actual reinstatement of Winchell as
part of the regular first night audience in the Shubert
houses came, according to Winchell, when Al Jolson
refused to go on at the opening of "Wunderbar" unless the producers let the flip critic in. This is the
same Mr. Jolson who in July, 1933, rose one evening
in Hollywood and knocked Winchell down twice
because, he said, word had reached him that Winchell's motion picture scenario, which he had just sold
for $25,000 ("Broadway Through a Keyhole") dealt
with the career of Mrs. Jolson (Ruby Keeler). Winchell said he regarded the incident as good publicity.

A frenzied worker, his health always has been good,
even if he did fall when the aging Jolson hit him. He
is neither profligate, boozy nor debauched. Soon after
the killing of Vincent Coll he announced that he had
had a breakdown, and took some time off. How serious this breakdown was remains a matter between
Winchell, the medical profession and God. He went
to California. Rumors reached him that stories were
being spread that he was dying, that he was paralyzed
in the left side, that he had been run out of New York

by gangsters, and so on.   It got under his skin and
he rushed back to New York.

His rise has been steady, and he has had a good time.
The only real tragedy in his life was the death in December, 1932, of his nine-year-old daughter, Gloria.
He has a younger daughter, Walda.   He had referred
to them many times in his column, and his friends
knew of his great devotion to his family.   Indeed,
one of the thousands of criticisms leveled at Winchell
at one time or another has been that he mentioned
his family too frequently.   Wherever a few people
are gathered together, they argue about whether Winchell transgresses good taste, and on Broadway no one
has ever drawn up a comprehensive code to define
good taste.

In the summer of 1933 Westbrook Pegler in the
New York *Evening Post* ran a column which he
called "A Sport Writer Interviews Himself," done
in the manner of Winchell's familiar "Portrait of a
Man Talking to Himself."   It combined, more nearly
than anything else, all the objections which have been
raised against Winchell's personality, taste and attitude.   It was reprinted in *Variety*, which had been
carrying on a desultory quarrel with Winchell. *Variety* prefaced the column with this comment:

"In Walter Winchell's inside coat pocket, carelessly
held in a card case, is a nice collection of soft soap
spilled over Winchell in the very nice way of Damon

Runyon. If Winchell can halt a bystander long enough, the victim is made to read the Runyon stuff on Winchell. Winchell enjoys it so much that he often asks the bystander to read it aloud, because Winchell can't believe his eyes.

"Westbrook Pegler has a nice way of writing, too. Thousands and thousands of newspaper readers have learned to think very highly of the Chicago *Tribune* syndicated writing ace.

"Mr. Pegler one day a few days ago wrote one of his daily columns. The Pegler column was about columnists. Pegler called it a sport writer talking to himself, but you have difficulty in recognizing any sport writer it fits. The first hasty conclusion is that the Pegler interview seems rather to fit a Broadway columnist, maybe any Broadway columnist.

"For fear Walter, me boy, failed to see Mr. Pegler's contribution it is here submitted, as it's quite well known in the night clubs of New York where stews assemble that Winchell's first crack Tuesday morning is:

" 'I wonder what that louse *Variety* has in this week about me.'

"With Winchell inviting some of the bystanders to read the Runyon essay over in person there's a chance he will also be informed just whom Mr. Pegler had in mind."

Pegler's column:

"Oh, how I love my beautiful, darling wife and kiddies. I am one of the best husbands in the world. And fathers, too. Some husbands and fathers keep these things in the bosom of the family, but it is a business with me, and I blab it all over good white paper.

"Hello, sweetheart. Here is a kiss for you. I am selling this kiss to the customers for three cents a copy; ten cents on Sundays. Don't forget to give little Shirley her spinach tonight. I have your photograph in the drawer beside me, darling. In my watch, too. Also in my hat. Hello, Shirley, darling. Your papa sends you a kiss. Your papa loves you. Papa loves baby. Isn't that original, darling?

"Sometimes I get disgusted when people think I am hard-boiled and blasé and cynical. People are always thinking about me. Oh, why does everybody think about me all the time? And why do people think I am conceited and stuck up when I am one of the most democratic and kind-hearted and family-loving people in all the world? Even if I am standing on the pinnacle of success, I am always willing to lend a helping hand to those who are strugglin' in the battle of life.

"This is the great humanitarian in me, although, to hear my enemies tell it, you wouldn't know it. I

used to be one of the humble class, myself, once, before I became so successful.

"But is it worth while to be a great man? Sometimes I wonder, darling.

"I must remember to write something nice about
George Washington. He deserves it, even from me.
Walnuts grow on trees. Shakespeare died at the age
of fifty.

"Rather clever, I thought. I mean what Izzy
Blotz, the featherweight fighter, said to the elevator
boy at the Garden the other night.

" 'Hello,' piped Blotz; 'I see you have your ups and
downs.'

"Wonder if it's true. I mean about what I mean.
I mean about the rumor what I mean. It certainly
will prove what I mean if I mean what I mean.

"A certain party has been writing poison pen letters about me. And the party is known. Jealous of
my success, that's all.

"I am so important that a great many people write
poison pen letters about me. But what they forget is
that I love my wife and kiddies.

"Hello, darling, here is another kiss for you (three
cents daily; ten cents on Sundays).

"My goodness, how the money rolls in.

"Oh, well, if you want to be an honest, fearless and
a big, outstanding success, you have to have a brave
bodyguard so you will not get slapped on the nose.

Bodyguards cost money, but when I need money I just kiss my darling wife and little Shirley in print and meet the payroll.

"Butch Butcher certainly is a grand guy and a true pal. One of the sweetest pals in the world. They call him a racketeer. The big bankers, that is. But they don't know what a grand guy and a true pal he is. While they are robbing the poor people, he robs the rich. They say he kicks his mother.

"But they don't tell you that he kicks her with his right foot. Butch is left-footed. Rope is made of hemp.

"I must remember to put the blast on Pontius Pilate. There was a dirty coward, if there ever was one. I am not afraid to speak out, let the chips fall where they may.

"That certainly was nice of President Roosevelt to write me that boosting letter telling me how much he liked my stuff. I wrote him, saying, 'I certainly hope you have a successful administration,' and he wrote back out of a clear sky, 'I cannot find words to express my opinion of your stuff.'

"What is life, after all? A guttering candle. A flickering flame. A cast of the dice. A wee deoch and doris.

"Hello, sweetheart, here is another kiss for you (three cents a copy today). Don't forget to give little Shirley her spinach, dear.

"Benedict Arnold certainly was a dirty bum.
"Henry the Eighth was a King of England.
"Goodnight, sweetheart."

Cruel business, and calculated to make Winchell's face red, but Broadway is not an overpolite place, and Winchell himself, for all his occasional acts of kindness to persons who have been treated unjustly, or who are out of work, has written many a line that caused pain—if not pain, then surely acute embarrassment.

Winchell is the perfect flower of Broadway, the product of his period as surely as prohibition and the night clubs and the tommy-guns. He is gay, and when he speaks the words come tumbling out as if he were thinking at the top of his voice and was barely able to contain his pent-up excitement. He is not fooled by Broadway any more than any other sane person is fooled by it. But he plays it for all it is worth, and the cash rolls in. He laid the ground for a horde of imitators, some good and some terrible, who are using his formula to depict the pageant of the great men, the beauties and the mountebanks of New York. A few of them do it expertly, but there is only one blown-in-the-bottle Winchell.

There are two schools of thought about his contribution to the period: one holds that he is important because he is a matchless reporter of human trivia;

the other contends that he deserves fame because of his additions to the language. Sometimes, in his efforts to surpass himself, he mauls and twists the English language to the straining-point, and even his best friends, whose ears are pretty well attuned to his nuances, don't know what he means.

His first and most popular phrase occurred in the oft-repeated announcement that Mr. and Mrs. So-and-So "anticipate a blessed event." Finally this became an outworn cliche, and Winchell and his imitators would write that the couple are "preparing a bassinet," "getting storked" or awaiting "a blessed expense." For couples who are not getting along so well, or preparing to separate, he has many descriptions. Sometimes they are "on the verge" and sometimes they are "straining at the handcuffs." Those who are to get divorces will "tell it to the judge" or be "Reno-vated." When people do things quietly they do it "sotto voce." Sometimes people are "Cupiding out loud," or they are "blazing again," or "on fire," or merely "that way." People drank "giggle water" and "made whoopee."

Collectors of Winchelliana are inclined to agree that his best line was "Those who live in tin houses shouldn't throw can-openers."

Winchell is Jewish, and he knows an eternal truth, discovered years ago by Montague Glass, that Jews like jokes on Jews. He is, indeed, on safer ground there than when he leans to the serious side of Jewish problems. Once, after he had flared up at some slur against the race, a prominent Jew said to him: "Please don't disgrace us by a defense, because you admit you are not a good Jew—because you haven't been in a synagogue since your confirmation—so, obviously, you know nothing about Jewry and you might be misunderstood."

Every time he hears a new Jewish joke that he thinks is worth repeating he prints it. Here is a sample of his jokes on the "dialecticians," as he calls them (when he doesn't say "herring-tearers"):

"For the tenth time the room clerk, with adenoids and an expression as though he were smelling something objectionable, insisted to Mr. Goldfarb that there were no rooms available at his ritzy hotel and that there was a waiting list ahead of him up to fifty years hence. And for the tenth time Mr. Goldfarb scratched the egg from his vest and insisted upon knowing the rates per day.

" 'Why,' why'd the stiff clerk, 'do you insist on knowing?'

" 'Becuz,' said the dialectician, 'furr saven mont's I'm paying here de rant for my baby-doll and I t'ink I'm bing geep'd hon de rates!' "

Mr. Goldfarb seldom appears. Usually the hero of his Jewish stories is a splendid composite character whom Winchell calls Mefoofsky.

Better than any of his gossiping contemporaries, Winchell, the ex-hoofer, caught the tempo of the New York of the twenties and the early thirties. That tempo was brittle, cheap, garish, loud, and full of wild dissonances. And he didn't really have to peep through a keyhole to find out what was going on. He couldn't have missed it blindfolded.

THE BULLS ARE LOOSE

THE average citizen believes, as a fixed part of his credo, that a large percentage of policemen are corrupt, venal and indolent. He always believed this, and he always had evidence for it. Before prohibition, the citizen knew that many a policeman would run the whole gamut of safe graft—from taking fruit from a pedler's cart to turning his back for a consideration when something serious was coming off.

Even so, back in those remote days, the citizen felt that the ordinary policeman, when life and property were threatened, was his friend. He might be stupid, this cop on the corner, but he was brave. Moreover, the public was indignant at evidences of official corruption among the higher police officers. The man in the street didn't like it when Lieutenant Charles Becker, protector of New York gambling houses, was disclosed as the instigator of Herman Rosenthal's murder. There was a great to-do, and not only Becker, but the four gunmen, the notorious Gyp the Blood, Lefty Louie, Dago Frank and Whitey Lewis, went to the electric chair. The public temper called for punishment.

There came, with prohibition, a subtle and sinister

change. To begin with, in the large cities, where the
sentiment was overwhelmingly opposed to the prohibition law, most of the so-called ordinary law-abiding
citizens were sympathetic toward most acts which
might tend to nullify the law. It was not long before
the police forces of the larger cities were being accused of complicity with politicians on the one hand
and bootleggers on the other, all for the purpose of
making liquor easier to get. It soon became common
knowledge to any observant citizen that the patrolman on the beat was taking cash and other favors
from speakeasy proprietors, drivers of beer trucks and
all that motley crew engaged in the circumvention of
an unpopular law. And there were, of course, strong
suspicions that sometimes the money reached higher
up.

Well, what of it? Wasn't it better for a cop to
take money from a bootlegger than from a prostitute?
Somehow it didn't seem so wrong. And surely it
wasn't as bad as conspiring to protect gambling houses
and yeggmen. And yet, the most competent diag-
nosticians of the police problems during the prohibition era have found that this very complacency, this
willingness to justify the taking of one form of graft,
caused a dangerous breakdown in the character, the
morale and the ethical senses of many an otherwise
excellent police force. The game grew too deep.
There were beer wars, hijackings and feuds between

rival gangs.   It was then that the cop found himself
in a tight spot.   He hasn't extricated himself yet;
more, he must go a long way to gain the public confidence.

It is true in Chicago, as it is true in New York,
that the average citizen wants to trust the police, but
he can't do it.   The administration usually is shot
through with politics of the worst sort; if not politics, then sheer incompetence.   Most policemen are
brave fellows, with a savage hatred of crooks, but
they are members of a system which often handcuffs
them.

Consider how Police Commissioners are made in
New York.   Let us take the classic example of John
F. Hylan, who became Mayor of New York on January 1, 1918.   Always amusing, Mr. Hylan began his
tenure, which was to last eight years, by grappling
with the police problem.   He had in office a rather
ineffectual man named Frederick H. Bugher, but he
wasn't sure what to do about it.   One night Hylan lay
tossing with his fitful dreams in the darkness of his
bedroom in the Bushwick section of Brooklyn.   At
the time the event was not made public; indeed, it was
five years later that Red Mike, as Hylan was affection-
ately known to the amused electorate of New York,
disclosed what had happened that night.   There came
a Voice.   Where from, no one knows, but it called insistently and with unmistakable authority, saying:

"Get rid of Bugher. He will make trouble. Enright—Enright is the man."

To hear a Voice was to act. Bugher, who had held
the office for only three weeks, was kicked out. His
place was taken by Richard E. Enright, a garrulous
and extremely ambitious police lieutenant. He had
a mop of curly gray hair, a bristling mustache, a
portly body and a tongue which could be both sharp
and eloquent. Some people called him Silver Dick.
He lasted eight years. Hylan, in the face of almost
universal criticism, stuck by Enright, who eventually
was replaced by what was regarded as the first genuinely constructive act of the new Mayor, James J.
Walker.

Thus, by Voices in the night, by the suggestion of a
newspaper reporter, by the desire to reward an old
friend, or the direct order of a political boss, a Police
Commissioner in New York is made or broken. The
wonder of it all is that the town now and then gets
a good one—even one who manages to keep his hands
clear of political chicanery. But the job is never easy.
Few of the good ones last long. The cop, always in
every city, is the whipping boy of the reformers.
Usually it is the most vulnerable of all city departments. Certainly, if the crusaders want to make it
seem so, the police department nearly always is open
to serious criticism. It may be brutality, or a particularly shocking unsolved murder, or bribery, or graft

in prostitution or gambling, or booze connections—
whatever it is, the police usually are open to attack.
The head of the department can't begin to please
everybody; few persons understand the nature of his
job, few know anything of the law, and a large number are suspicious of the cops on general principles.

New Yorkers, however, have a curious sense of civic
pride. They can tolerate the most outlandish extrav-
agances, even graft on a large scale, but they retain a
certain childish fondness for the police force as a
whole. They like to watch the handsome young men
in their annual parade up Fifth Avenue.

The department in New York now has, roughly,
20,000 men. In recent years the recruits have been
of an excellent quality, and well trained. Moreover,
the rush of young men of high qualifications to join
the force is greater than ever before; when Theodore
Roosevelt was Commissioner he felt impelled to send
out a call for a better type of man. The police are
hampered quite a bit by Tammany interference,
though probably not as much as most persons profess
to believe. Certainly politics is not so noticeable as
in the days of Chief William S. Devery.

Promotion in the department, ordinarily, is pretty
much on solid merit, and it takes study, intelligence
and definite ability to pass examinations for the higher
ranks. Of recent years, particularly since Enright
went out of the Commissionership, there has been an

astonishing improvement in the attitude of the New York policeman toward the plain citizen. Most of them now are, within reason, courteous. Physically the force is admirable. As for brains, few of them are notable, but they have come a long way from the old-time sodden, surly flatfoot.

Some admirer long ago called the New York police "The Finest." Perhaps they are, but everyone knows that in such a large group there are all sorts—brave fellows and craven thieves, rounders and studious husbands, drunken bullies and men who could be trusted in any circumstances. From "The Finest" one may cull some appalling examples of crookedness. Two of them recently were caught for helping some gangsters kidnap a bootlegger and hold him for ransom. When the suspicion grew strong among the seventeen detectives working on the case that members of the department were involved, they went after the case with tremendous fury, gave the two crooks an artistic going-over and did much to increase public confidence in detective work.

The decent policemen (and they must be overwhelmingly in the majority) have their hands full in cities like New York and Chicago. New York probably is infested with as savage a horde of cut-throats, rats, treacherous gunmen and racketeers as ever swarmed upon a rich and supine principality. Some of them are of high intelligence, and are so rich, and so clever, and so well protected by the intricate machinery which they have built up for themselves, that it is next to impossible for the police to do anything with them. Worse than Chicago? That would be hard to say. Certainly the city of Capone and the pineapples, which gave to criminal history the all but unbelievable St. Valentine's Day Massacre, has the more lurid reputation. But there is much to be said for New York; for all around thuggery, even for the number of persons who were taken for rides, the New York bad men have been able to hold their own. The Chicago press, it may be, has been more assiduous in printing crime news than the New York press, and, in particular, has built up the reputations of certain highly entertaining underworld characters.

All this is not to say that New York is in a constant turmoil of killings, bombings, snatchings, rapine and pillage. The ordinary citizen can go through life, sometimes, drinking his booze, working his heart out at his job, paying his bills and his taxes, without ever having any close dealings either with the police or the flaming lords of the underworld. However, there is no sense in attempting to deny that the city, always the symbol of evil to the outlanders, is made up of some of the most reckless, perverted and conscienceless mugs that ever were spawned. The most evil city in the world? It all depends on where you look. Port Said and Marseilles and Harbin have reputations,

but there are spots in New York which surely reach
close to the lowest in depravity.

One street is so dangerous that the police warn even
moderately well-dressed men not to walk through it
in broad daylight. New York has a type of gunman
who would shoot his grandmother in the back and lay
bets on which way she would fall. There are brothels
which are said by students to be the most astonishing
things since Babylon. One day the telephone of the
manager of a hotel in the West Forties rang and a
voice announced: "Tell that rat in Room 929 that
I'm coming over tonight and that I'm going to cut
his heart out and throw it in his face." The manager,
who was new at that hotel, laughed it off as some sort
of pleasantry. He was somewhat shaken the next
morning when he found that the threat had been carried out exactly as announced.

New York, in its worst spots, never did have a
reputation of excessive purity, but after prohibition
these bad spots assumed a vastly more complicated
and serious aspect. Bank robbers, murderers, bomb-
throwers, confidence men and all stripes of racketeers
began taking an interest in booze. They had an interest in night clubs and speakeasies where nice people
thought they had to go to have a good time. Time
and again it has been shown that police officers either
were in the pay of such places, or were friendly with
the owners, or had some vague connection which

would have made it embarrassing for them to proceed against the joints.

Not much has been done about it, and probably not much ever will be done. The sporadic "drives" and "curfews" usually are so much window dressing. New York, with its eager, fun-loving visitors added to the local population of playboys, wants alcohol and amusement, and, as always, among the purveyors of amusement will be some harpies.

There was once a great Mayor of New York, William J. Gaynor, who knew the law as well as the temper of the people of his city. It was Gaynor who recommended that the duty of the police was to preserve "outward order and decency"—a sensible ideal which often is forgotten by politicians and policemen, and nearly always by the uplifters. About the best that New Yorkers, or the citizens of any other large city, can hope for is that the more glaring crimes will be punished promptly, that the cop found grafting will be kicked off the force, and that the political bosses will keep at the head of the department a man in whom the people have some degree of confidence.

Although the idea never was put forward officially, it is perfectly true that what the law enforcement bodies of the large cities wanted during the prohibition era was not enforcement but a sort of safe regulation of the liquor-selling traffic. The ideal was for everybody to be able to have a drink—but quietly and even surreptitiously. The accusation was made over and over by such dry leaders as Mrs. Ella A. Boole, Bishop James Cannon, Jr., and Fred A. Victor of the Anti-Saloon League of New York, that the police could dry up New York if they wanted to. Out of all the welter of curious statements made by these people during their long and losing battle, this statement contains a good deal of truth.

The great William Travers Jerome, now retired and wealthy, emerged from the silences long enough in 1929 to comment upon the complaint of Grover A. Whalen, then Police Commissioner, that there were appalling numbers of speakeasies in New York and that they were "breeding-places for criminals."

"Bosh!" snorted Jerome. "Mr. Whalen could close them all up in thirty days if he wanted to. If he couldn't he has no business being Police Commissioner. There can't be a speakeasy open up anywhere in this town without the cop on the beat knowing about it in a week. And then his captain knows too. If he doesn't he's no captain."

Mr. Jerome's opinion was relayed to several thoughtful speakeasy proprietors, men who had been in the business of selling booze for many years. They disagreed with him; the job could be done, thoroughly and absolutely, in twenty-four hours. Turned loose, knowing that their superior officers were back of them, and without being too careful about the strict letter of the law, the gendarmes of New York could have shut the place so tight that Emporia, Kansas, would have looked like a hot spot in comparison. Perhaps the job would have taken a week, but it could have been done. Who wanted it done? No one, except the dry crusaders, and even they would have been out of jobs if it had been done.

God knows the cop on the beat is not in favor of prohibition. He knows that a glass of beer, or a gin rickey, or even a shot of Scotch, is of infinite help in easing his aching feet and his harassed mind. The policeman, for all his petty infirmities, is like other men at heart. He will sympathize with his pals, he will even sock the enemies of his pals, and he is grateful for small favors and meaningless flatteries. He, too, has his griefs, his troubles with women and money; and occasionally he has his thwarted dreams.

And the doings of the cops are amusing without end. Even the uniformed patrolmen, called harness bulls by the unthinking, have their moments of charm. And one could pick a dozen detectives whose lunch or dinner conversation would make more sense, and be much funnier, than any of the sessions of the Algonquin Round Table.

It will be found that the policeman is uniformly courageous when facing great physical danger, that he is likely to turn his back on a possibly fatal encounter when he is sure it is none of his business, that he has a brutal contempt for the lower class of criminal, that he regards small change received from certain sources for favors rendered as perfectly legitimate, that he will stick by a friend and lie his head off if necessary when the friend is in a jam, that he laps up goose grease and even the cruder forms of blandishment, that he always has one or more favorite wrongdoers who he insists are all right, that he is impressed deeply by persons of great wealth or social position. That is to say, when you cut him, he bleeds; when you starve him, he howls.

A few of the New York police have almost Homeric achievements to their credit. There is, for example, Detective William Quaine of the East 104th street station, which embraces what is perhaps the toughest district in the city—a district containing the conglomeration of many races, bitten by poverty and ridden by rackets and assorted types of gangs. The good people there swear by Quaine, who for many years has conducted what amounts to a fierce one-man crusade against criminals. Scores of times his life has been in danger; attempts to assassinate him have been many; the superstitious among the gunmen believe it is impossible to kill him; he, by the records, has earned the reputation of being the toughest detective in the city, tougher even than the famous Johnny Broderick. He has been accused of excessive brutality, of using extra-legal methods; but he is up against an element which understands nothing else. Every one of Quaine's fingers has been broken. And yet this man has found employment for hundreds of former convicts and for potential criminals who he thought might go straight. And he has been caught teaching algebra to little Italian children.

As an example of what may happen to a police officer, no matter how innocent may have been his intentions, when he mixes business with pleasure, there was the celebrated case of Detective Albert C. Johnson, who was a guest at a dinner given to Magistrate Albert H. Vitale in the Roman Gardens on the night of December 7, 1929. At 1:30 in the morning seven men entered and robbed fifty-three of the sixty guests of jewelry valued at $2,500, along with $2,000 in cash. The dinner was given by the Tepecano Democratic Club, out of whose membership of three hundred there were twenty-eight whose pictures hung in the Rogues' Gallery at Police Headquarters. The secret service squad of the police contended that the robbery was a fake arranged by Ciro Terranova, known as the artichoke king, to regain a contract held by a Chicago gunman for the killing of Frank Uale and Frank Marlow, but they couldn't prove it. And the unfortunate Detective Johnson found himself in hot water. He was fined thirty days' pay and put back in the uniform of a patrolman after he had been found guilty of associating at a social affair with crim-

inals, of failing to report promptly on the robbery, of
entering a place on the suspect list, and of carelessness
in betraying to the robbers that he had a pistol, which
had been taken from him. At last reports Johnson
had been promoted to headquarters.

Most detectives like to associate with prominent
persons. One evening there was a dinner and reception at the home of one of the world's wealthiest men
to celebrate the wedding of the man's son. Police
Headquarters had been asked to send a squad of
picked men to guard the guests and the baubles. A
dozen or so of the most handsome detectives arrived
in evening clothes and carried out their duties perfectly. As the party was breaking up the secretary
of the great man offered the leader of the group ten
dollars as an honorarium. "If I had taken it and tried
to divide it among the boys they would have thought
I was holding out on them," he confided later. He
sent the bewildered secretary, who didn't know that
if there was to be any payment at all it should be
something more substantial, from one detective to
another, but they all spurned the money. Then, in a
howling rage because they had wasted an evening in
their fine clothes for nothing, the detectives rushed to
a place in West Forty-eighth Street to forget their
wounds. The bill there came to twelve dollars per
detective. The detectives asked the Commissioner the

next day to excuse them for a while from similar assignments; it was too expensive.

The police rarely liked to conduct a raid on a high-class speakeasy, and usually did so only when the Commissioner received specific complaints from citizens who felt they had been treated unfairly in such places. There was one raid on the complaint of a powerful neighbor. Some of the police got behind the onyx bar and acted as bartenders for an hour or so, departing finally with some of the liquor they had found in the place. The establishment opened for business as usual as soon as the police left, with plenty of liquor brought down from the enormous reserve supply upstairs. Nobody cared, least of all the police. But the place, nevertheless, had been "raided."

Whatever else may have been said of James J. Walker's administration as Mayor, he usually tried to have a man at the head of the Police Department who would not bring down the wrath of the reformers, the Republicans and the newspapers. When he resigned his office, a tired and lovesick little man, after his inept and halting defense before Governor Franklin D. Roosevelt, he had little to apologize for in the conduct of the Police Department. He apparently wanted to keep the force as clean as it could be kept. He knew, as any bright lawyer-politician reared in New York couldn't help knowing, that the hounds of Heaven, once given the scent, will bay first at the cops.

The men selected by Walker to head the department were George V. McLaughlin, a banker and a hard man, stubborn and implacable, who finally quit the job because the Tammany district leaders complained so much about his raids on their clubhouses for gambling; Joseph A. Warren, Walker's former law partner, a well-meaning, gentle little man who quit when it became apparent that he had neither the stomach nor the stamina for the job; Grover A. Whalen, the great front man, the department store executive who made welcoming an art and who put more showmanship in the department than one will find in the Delhi Durbar; and, finally, Edward P. Mulrooney, who had been a policeman all his life and who resigned in the spring of 1933 to become chairman of the State Alcoholic Beverage Control Commission.

When Enright was Commissioner under Hylan, the complaint was frequent that it was bad policy to have a man from the force on the job. This point of view may be upheld by many powerful arguments. For one thing, such a man usually wants to settle old scores. He is likely to be too much the cop, and to have too little regard for the currents of public opinion. Under Mulrooney, who was Commissioner for three years, there was no such complaint. Although certain types of crime increased while he was in office,

sioner, under the late Mayor John Purroy Mitchel, said that "the gangster and the gunman are practically extinct." This at a time when every sign—the break-up of the old-time gangs, the special problems of wartime and the approach of prohibition—pointed to the spawning of mobs of gorillas beside whom the pre-war thugs appear as amiable but fairly harmless roughnecks. Enright, at a time when everyone knew that the bandits of New York were going into action on all fronts, made speeches in which he said that the "crime wave" was purely an invention of the press, which, for some reason not made clear, had been forced by certain unidentified interests in Wall Street to foster the libel of increased crime and injure the hitherto fair name of the city. Whalen got in bad with the faint hearts when he said that there was a lot of law in the end of a nightstick, probably a correct enough observation, but injudicious. Indeed, almost all heads of Police Departments, in whatever city, appear to have the wholly unlegal theory that it is the duty of the police to punish crime. The police still usurp the functions of the courts in that they use fists, blackjacks, revolvers and other instruments, but there is another side to it—ask any realistic old-time police captain how to keep a district clean.

To Mr. Whalen, with whom Mr. Mulrooney served as head of the detectives, goes much of the credit for

making the New York police more attractive in dress
and appearance and more courteous. Time was when
few policemen would give a citizen an answer to a
single question without snarling. Perhaps Whalen's
worst mistake in psychology was in his handling of
the interminable gatherings of the obstreperous Communists. There were many head-crackings and pho-
tographs of mounted policemen, all of which delighted Moscow and was exactly what the Reds were
after. Under Mulrooney the police were firm but
amazingly patient with such gatherings.

Most critics of the police in the big cities are fond
of saying that there has been little or no change in
police methods from the period of forty or fifty years
ago, when the principal job of the patrolman was the
subjugation of the loud-mouthed drunk. This is
hardly true. The science of criminal identification
has been developed to a remarkably efficient degree.
The undercover or secret service squads often are able
to prevent crimes and trap criminals. The police
themselves are better educated and more adaptable.
The handling of traffic has reached the point almost
of an exact science. One of the most effective inno-
vations under Mulrooney was the organization of a
radio alarm system, by means of which tremendous
man-power, fast police cars equipped with radios and
loaded with sharpshooting policemen, can be brought

quickly to any spot where trouble is reported.   This
scheme doesn't catch them all (witness the escape of
the two automobiles loaded with gunmen who raced
down Broadway in the spring of 1933, machine-guns
spurting at each other), but its value already has been
made clear enough.

Of course the most shocking aspect of crime in
America, the aspect which surely attracts the most
attention and which makes this nation appear so bizarre to the lethargic English, is the failure of the
police to solve the murders of well-known underworld
figures.   If detective science is worth anything at all,
why aren't more of these cases cleared up?

In Chicago the list, published over and over before
the advent of the Century of Progress, is a nightmare
of blood.   In New York the list likewise is bad
enough.   To name a few: Frankie Uale, the Sicilian
leader who was shot down in Brooklyn in a plot which
had its ramifications in Chicago and Florida; Arnold
Rothstein, the gambler who was found mortally
wounded after a conference in a hotel room, and
whose killer still is the subject of hot debates in the
barrooms of New York, one school of thought sticking to one man and another to an entirely different
person; Jerge the dope pedler, shot down in an automobile in Broadway near the Metropolitan Opera
House on a quiet Sunday afternoon; Vannie Higgins,

tough booze runner, murdered outside a dance-hall
in Brooklyn; Vincent Coll, the wild, gat-goofy youth
who was mowed down by a machine-gun in a telephone booth; Joe Masseria, the celebrated Joe the
Boss, whose violent ending might have been brought
about for any one of a number of reasons; Frankie
Marlow, whose real name was Curto, lured from a restaurant in the West Fifties and taken for his final
drive into Kings County, where his body was dumped
out near a cemetery.

And there are many others, big and little. To be
sure, in some instances the police know perfectly well
who did it, but they are unable to get proof which
would mean anything in court. Most of the more
prosperous mob leaders, despite their ignorance and
uncouthness, have developed a cunning which makes
them almost immune to prosecution.

In all truth, the police do not always search very
assiduously for the killers. Officially, the police heads
point out that murder is murder, and that they in-
tend to get at the bottom of the case if possible.
Actually and confidentially, the police attitude frequently is this: "Let them be their own executioners.
We are not really looking for So-and-So. The boys
will take care of him." And, as predicted, the boys
frequently do finish the job.

Such an attitude is indefensible in law and ethics,

but it is secretly condoned by many realistic citizens. It is an attitude which is a natural product of the problems of prohibition. The profits of alcohol not only attracted the former pickpocket, the payroll robber, the burglar and the forger, but it also attracted other types of men, some of whom had brains.

What are the police doing with these men now? With the legalization of 3.2% beer in 1933 there came a dangerous shift in the alignment of the underworld forces. Many of the speakeasy proprietors who for years had depended upon the drinkers of hard liquor for their profits found that most of their customers had deserted them for the beer places. What to do? Some of them sold both beer and hard liquor openly—an illegal practise but one which can be continued indefinitely with the right sort of protection.

Worse, despite the elaborate licensing and inspection precautions provided for under the New York state beer law, and despite the presence of the honest and conscientious Mulrooney as head of the board, it was not long before reports were all over the East telling of how organizations of gangsters were "turning legitimate" and getting control of breweries, organizing sales organizations to force retailers to buy their products, buying up chains of beer gardens, "cutting in" on kegs and distribution arrangements.

The bonanza of the prohibition era came from the

sale of alcohol. The more intelligent leaders of the underworld (and they don't have to be too bright at that) are perceiving that alcohol, even with repeal and strict laws for manufacture, distribution and retail, will still be a source of income—perhaps greater than ever. Surely, although some of the underworld will go back to the older and rougher pursuits, they would prefer to remain in the liquor business and to have a hand in the multitude of interlocking rackets which the legalization of booze may make possible.

What to do about it? It is not a job for the cop on his beat; that brave fellow will go on getting his free shot of rye, eventually a bullet in his belly and his name on the tablet of heroes at Police Headquarters. It is a job for Washington in the control of the interstate aspects of liquor running and rackets; for the police administrations of the cities, and for the prosecutors.

These last, the District Attorneys' offices in the larger centers of population, need a thorough overhauling. In only one of the five counties which make up New York City has there been anything resembling a fierce, well-directed intention to end rackets. That is in Bronx County, where, somehow, the District Attorney for several years has been able to keep awake. In New York County, where men like William Travers Jerome and Charles S. Whitman once raised the roof, the District Attorney at the beginning of the New Deal was Thomas C. T. Crain, the gentle, septuagenarian Sachem of Tammany Hall—a poodle set to bring down hyenas.

THE LAST DRAGON-SLAYER

THE Rev. John Roach Straton, a strident orator and a tricky fighter, was the bellwether of the Fundamentalists and the darling of New York for eleven years. He was the last crusader. When he died, broken by the fury of his tour of the South against Al Smith, there was no one among the reformers who could replace him, either as an influence or as an amusing figure.

New York, to the unflinching Straton, was not a city to be enjoyed, or tolerated, or laughed at, but a hell-hole to be saved from its own voluptuous self. His Jehovah was personal, and so was his Devil. He preached the old-time religion, and his theory of life was built upon the simple, Spartan virtues.

In the days when Patrick Cardinal Hayes of the Catholics, Rabbi Stephen S. Wise of the Jews, Bishop William T. Manning of the Episcopalians, the Rev. Dr. Christian Fichthorne Reisner of the Methodists, and the Rev. Dr. Harry Emerson Fosdick of the Modernist, or Rockefeller, wing of the Baptists, were carrying out their ecclesiastical duties according to their own faiths and their own judgment, seldom making any untoward uproar against anything except the ordinary sins which have beset the human race since antiquity, Dr. Straton was fighting all comers.

He did not stop when he had said a harsh word against such standard crimes as murder, arson, rape and robbery. In his time he inveighed against card playing, cocktail drinking, poodle dogs, jazz music, the theater, low-cut dresses, divorce, novels, stuffy rooms, Clarence Darrow, overeating, the Museum of Natural History, evolution, the Standard Oil influence in the Baptist church, prizefighting, the private lives of actors, nude art, bridge playing, modernism and greyhound racing.

He made of himself, according to one's viewpoint, either a great preacher, a metropolitan circus, or a genuine menace to all that liberal-minded men hold dear. In New York, a city reeking with hell-bound cynics, he was laughed at, but he got an enormous lot of publicity. They did not clearly understand that his views were held by millions outside of New York, and that Straton himself was a symbol of righteousness to the rest of dry, Puritan America. In the oil-lamp circuits in the South they swore by him.

It was in 1918, after he had tilted against sin in Norfolk and Baltimore, that he came to Calvary Baptist Church, in West Fifty-seventh street, New York, to replace the aged and beloved Rev. Dr. MacArthur. The city heard a new voice—a voice reminiscent of the nights when Billy Sunday, Dowie, Finney and

Moody had tried to save New York from a certain hell.

First, Straton denounced the users of roulette wheels in the sale of war savings stamps as "gamblers, felons and debauchers of the young." He criticized the Bal Bleu, a charity affair given by women of society at the Ritz-Carlton, as "an expression of paganism." One woman, rather sweetly, suggested that perhaps the doctor, having come only recently from Norfolk, was not accustomed to seeing women in evening dress. The doughty pastor, descendant of the Black Douglases of Scotland, retorted: "I was at a dinner party, not a great while ago, and sat next to a lady who was so scantily attired that I positively blushed when another gentleman came and stood at the back of my chair to say something to me." The man was not to be fooled. He knew a mammal when he saw one.

Next he went to see "Aphrodite" at the Century Theater, a production which, for those days, was regarded as pretty far south. He reported: "It was a nightmare of nude men and women who were slobbering over each other and lolling on couches with each other, and dancing in feigned drunken revelry together. What possible art or entertainment can there be in the silly cavorting of harlots and degenerates?"

Some people were amused, but he got under the

there," demanded Straton, "and look upon the spectacle of two practically naked men, battering and bruising each other and struggling in sweat and blood for mere animal mastery?"

Straton came out in favor of legislation which would prohibit all public dancing except the more seemly sort of mazurkas, such as were danced by David and other pious hoofers in the olden times. Indeed, he was opposed to virtually everything in the way of amusement that was going on in New York.

Early in 1920, after National Prohibition had been in effect only a short time, he began his greatest and silliest crusade against the purely local manifestations of evil. Word had come to him that prohibition was not being enforced; indeed, he had heard, and accurately, that the town was full of gin-mills. Accompanied by Harry P. Burton, a newspaper man, and Daniel Hoffheim, of the old vice-chasing Committee of Fourteen, Dr. Straton disguised himself, with considerable difficulty, as a lover of fleshly pleasures, and hell-for-leather rounder, and made a tour of dance-halls, restaurants, speakeasies and other sindens on the West Side. Burton paid the bills.

In his pulpit the next Sunday Dr. Straton, apparently taking a leaf from the book of the more puissant Dr. Charles H. Parkhurst of another period of reform, preached a sermon in which he described New York as "a feverish, overwrought, Sabbathdesecrating, God-defying, woman-despising, law-breaking, gluttonous monster without ideals or restraint." He told of his peregrinations in the dreary hideaways of the damned, where he had met drunken women, prostitutes, dancing instructors whom he had adjudged to be of easy virtue, and other sad types of hellions. He said he had bought Scotch highballs in many places and that brothels existed with the knowledge and consent of the police.

Several arrests followed in the police district commanded by Inspector Dominick Henry. These raids were made over Henry's head and Henry was indicted for neglect of duty. The Inspector, whose best friends never accused him of being a mental giant, went through this puzzling period with a hurt, what-the-hell? expression on his Irish face, and eventually he was freed.

Among those arrested were Peter Galliotti and a waiter in Peter's place, and Thomas Healy, an old-time Broadway figure, in another resort. Straton was the chief witness against the prisoners charged with selling liquor when they were brought before United States Commissioner Hitchcock.

"You say you were served with a Scotch highball?" the pastor was asked. "Now, did you ever in your life taste Scotch whisky?"

"No," said Straton, and Hitchcock ruled that the preacher was an incompetent witness. Peter and

Thomas were freed. Straton had been trapped rather neatly, and had not been quick enough to tell the whole story in court of his knowledge of booze. It was therefore in the nature of an attempt to cover up that he announced in a subsequent sermon:

"I drank whisky when I was in college and afterward I drank it to cure colds. I know what whisky tastes like, and I tasted each of the drinks served to us in the places we visited. I simply took enough to convince myself that the stuff was whisky. One would not have to swallow a polecat to know it was a polecat."

But the damage was done, and the failure of this crusade weakened Straton's standing as a potential mopper-up of the booze joints. From that time on he devoted most of his talents to the fight against evolution.

At the time of the Scopes trial in Tennessee Straton was held in readiness by William Jennings Bryan as an expert witness whose testimony could demolish the whole tottering structure of evolution. "I am ready to come at the drop of a hat," Straton wired Bryan; but the hat never dropped.

Straton went to the Museum of Natural History and got into an argument with Dr. William K. Gregory, curator of the department of comparative anatomy. He contended that the museum, with an exhibit of skulls in the Hall of the Age of Man, was

poisoning the minds and corrupting the morals of
children. The exhibit, he said, "is treason to God
Almighty and a libel on the human race." Dr. Gregory argued long and patiently, but to no purpose.
Between him and Straton, he said, there was "a vast
gulf." Indeed there was. Although Straton could
denounce evolution for hours on end, he admitted
once, when brought down to cases, that he never had
read either Darwin, Spencer, Huxley, Bergson or the
modern Haldane.

From all over America the Fundamentalists came
to Straton's church, the believers from the little towns
who had been reared on the same theology that Straton
preached. These people preferred Straton to Fosdick,
the eloquent Modernist who in 1924 had been described by Straton, in his accustomed forthright fashion, as "a Baptist bootlegger, a Presbyterian outlaw,
and the Jesse James of the theological world." He
called John D. Rockefeller, Jr., whose money did
most to build Fosdick's great Riverside Church, "a
self-complacent and somnolent Modernist."

Straton, in West Fifty-seventh Street, seemed a
curious anachronism. There was, when he was powerful there, a hotel across the street, and a studio
building where artists went about their ungodly, suspicious business. A few doors away at least two dancing schools instructed the young in an art which
Straton frowned upon. More than one woman, said

to have been no better than she should have been, lived in the neighborhood. Sometimes gunmen popped at each other, taxicabs backed and filled, and fire engines shrieked. On the more quiet nights one could stand, very late, on the steps of Calvary and hear snatches of the music from the Club Richman and the Creole Follies.

And yet Straton, set down in this nest of evil, among a people who did not understand what he was driving at, and who regarded him as a querulous old man, sometimes amusing but most of the time a nuisance, continued his fight through the years. At times there were minor indications that he was softening, that he actually was beginning to mellow and to feel the charm of New York. He had a horse named Bob (the outside of a horse is the best thing for the inside of a man, he used to say) which he would ride along the bridle-paths of Central Park. His congregation gave him an automobile and he liked to drive. Once a glimmer of affection for the life of the city crept out, when he said:

"While God has laid it upon my heart to warn New York concerning the evils that are menacing her, nevertheless I have come to love this great and noble city."

If it was love, then it was the love which a stern, harsh father has for a son whom he regards as sinning. But all this was gibberish to most of New York. The man found it hard to unbend. Even his ordinary statements in conversation, such as, "I think I shall put another log on the fire," had about them a pious ponderosity which made them sound like the premonitory rumblings of the crack of doom.

His description of his conception of Heaven, used over and over in his sermons with only slight variations as to detail, was an eloquent passage which only led to the bewilderment of most New Yorkers. Here is Straton's idea:

"But think, my friends, what Heaven will be! . . . Stand yonder with me below the Arch of Triumph in Fifth Avenue and let us give play to our imaginations. Instead of that graceful arch being composed of man's poor plaster, which is already cracking and falling in decay, think of it as carved from one perfect opal or one giant diamond, fairly stabbing the eyes with the dazzling beauty of a million rays of light. And beyond it, reaching far and away, see the avenue, not with the cold drab stones that we know, but paved with pure gold so rare and fine that it shines like transparent glass. And there beside that matchless highway see trees with many-colored flowers, each bearing the fruits of life and the leaves that are for the healing of the nations, and to the right and left of these, as far as our wondering eyes can see, behold mansions of glory, built of opals and sapphires, and rubies, and pearls, planned by the skill of omnipotent

wisdom and executed by the power of a divine architect. Add to that little glimpse which the imagination gives a thousandfold increase in beauty and
sweetness and let the city stretch out and out, with its
jeweled walls fifteen hundred miles in each direction,
and its exquisite beauties piled plain on plain and
street above street, soaring up fifteen hundred miles
toward the eternal blue. Try with your poor finite
minds to think of that and to dream of it and you will
begin to catch some faint, far-off suggestion of the
place that God Almighty is preparing for them who
love Him!"

That place, which seemed rococo and uncomfortable to New Yorkers who were to become accustomed
to the Central Park Casino, the Empire State Building and the buildings of Rockefeller Center, was the
Heaven which Dr. Straton held up to the faithful.
How much he was carried away by his own eloquence
is something that no one can say, but it is likely that
he believed in a Heaven like that, as he believed the
Bible from cover to cover, and as he was sincere even
when he was making charges against people and institutions which most of his contemporaries regarded as
too sensational and even downright unfair.

He was no Elmer Gantry. Even his enemies, and
he tried the patience of many who knew him, never
found anything in his private life which would have
embarrassed his most strait-laced follower. If, in his

gyrations and his furious charges against what he regarded as the sins of New York, he reminded some
observers of the old meshuggah prophets of the desert,
that does not mean that he was not sincere.

He came from the Scottish border breed—a race
which may produce a hard drinker, a political wizard,
a smart confidence man, a hell-roaring evangelist or a
witch burner. Many of them have backbones of steel.
Such men usually amount to something. Straton received most of his schooling in the South, though he
was born in Indiana. When he was reminded once
that he was not in the Social Register he replied:

"Perhaps I can't qualify under the rules of your
pork-packing aristocracy. But I am descended from
the Black Douglases of Scotland and the Carters of
Virginia."

He attended Mercer University, hatchery of many
Southern preachers, and the Southern Baptist Theological Seminary at Louisville. Later he went to the
Boston School of Oratory. He schooled himself in all
the tortuous tricks of theological discourse and, although he had little use for the so-called higher criticism, he knew his Bible. He loved elocution and "expression." He memorized ancient, almost pointless
"nice" anecdotes and dressed them up until he was in
demand as a lecturer through the towns of the South
and Southwest. One lecture, delivered for a modest
fee, dealt with the glories of a chicken dinner; an-

other was on young married people and their heart-breaks, with comic overtones.

He might have made an excellent lawyer of the old school; indeed, he studied law for a time when he was eighteen years old and was working in the State Capitol in Atlanta. For the rest of his life he loved to tell of the unregenerate youth who had been "swept away from his moorings of faith" and who was "steeped in sin, loving sin." He drank some in those days, with an especial fondness for blackberry wine. And he played poker. Then he became religious one night while under the spell of the Rev. J. B. Hawthorne, one of the great evangelists of the time. From that time on he was a pulpit orator.

Already, in 1928, some of his friends thought they noticed a slackening of the old fire. He had been through some bitter fights with the anti-Straton element in his church, some of whom had alleged in court that it was not safe to allow him to handle the finances of the church—not that he was personally dishonest, but that he wasn't so good at figures. For years he had been wanting to tear down the old church structure and put up a modern, combined church, hotel and auditorium. He had won all these fights, but at terrible cost.

For ten years he had been hard at it in New York, and what had it got him? True, he had a comfortable enough life, but on all the charts giving the trends of

the times, sin was on the increase. People were making fortunes in Wall Street and spending them on
women, liquor and all the other outlets of a feverish
and moneyed civilization. Divorces were on the increase; so were murders and juvenile crime. People
weren't going to church any more; some churches reported that the percentage of new members was less
than it had been for one hundred years. So this was
what all the striving had been about, and this was the
result of a decade of fighting for righteousness in the
stronghold of the Prince of Darkness. In those days
his voice took on a petulant note and became harsh.

Then something happened which gave him new
hope, and a new chance. He always had been opposed to Al Smith, putting it principally on the
ground that Al was wet. Straton at one time and
another had been suspected of Ku-Klux Klan leanings,
and indeed he had given aid and comfort to at least
one Klan organizer. He always insisted, however,
that he was not in accord with all the Klan prejudices.
In particular, he said, he did not share their antipathy
toward Catholics, who, he felt, were an exceptionally
sensible lot, especially in their system of parochial
schools and denominational colleges.

Smith had been nominated for President and was
out to make a bitter fight, win or lose. One Sunday
Straton devoted his sermon to Smith, picturing him as
the spearhead of the forces of evil. What he actually

said was little different from what he had said a hundred times before, and to which neither Smith nor
anyone else had paid much attention. But this time
Smith, who was not disposed to countenance any
more attacks from Protestant pulpits, caught up Straton sharply and demanded that that doctor debate
him in Straton's own church.

Straton was delighted at the prospect, although, on
second thought, neither he nor Smith liked the idea
of debating in Calvary Church. Straton suggested
Madison Square Garden. No, even better, why not a
tour of the country, Straton versus Smith, putting on
the act in all the populous centers. It would be the
best show of the campaign. Smith perceived he was
dealing with a strange fellow, and the whole matter
fell through, with Straton explaining that he thought
Smith, personally, was a good man. Soft soap, for all
of Smith's ideas were anathema to the doctor.

With the chance gone to lift himself to a national
parity with the fighting Governor during the Presidential campaign, Straton, determined to make one
last stand, announced that he would tour the Southern States, taking the stump as often as possible to
denounce Al Smith, Tammany and the liquor traffic.
Years before, when a young man, he had won a prize
for a monograph on "the mental, moral, physical and
economic cost of the liquor traffic," which he had entitled "The Deadly Upas Tree." The Anti-Saloon

League had paid him $500 for it. Before he set out
on his tour he visited some of the newspaper offices in
New York and urged them to reprint this monograph
in full as part of the ballyhoo for his campaign against
Smith. When told that it couldn't be done, that it
was old stuff, he accused the editors of being friendly
to the liquor traffic; indeed, later, in a speech in
Georgia, he said that one of the editors who had refused to reprint his work had been drinking at the
time he made the refusal. This editor, a young man
renowned among his fellows for his almost unnatural
abstemiousness, was so hurt when he heard of this that
he broadcast damaging material on Straton to his
friends among the pro-Smith faction in the South.

On Straton went, from the Carolinas almost to the
borders of New Mexico, telling rapt audiences his
version of the life and times of Alfred E. Smith. To
be sure, Smith would have lost those states anyway
that year, but the fierce voice of Straton, one of the
many which were lifted in the same cause, did its
share in beating Smith.

He came back to New York, and the winter after
Smith's defeat little was heard of him. He was busy
on the details of his skyscraper church, but much of
the old fire was gone. Smith, as always, was a hero in
New York. In April, 1929, Straton suffered a slight
stroke. He went back to Atlanta, the city where he
had known sin as a youth, and where the miracle of

his regeneration had occurred, to rest. In the early fall he came back to New York, tired and shaky. He went to a sanitarium at Clifton Springs, New York. He died there at 5:30 o'clock on the morning of October 29, 1929.

He was only fifty-four years old when he died, but for years he had appeared much older than his real age. There is little doubt that the terrible campaign of hatred into which he threw himself in 1928 took all of his strength. True, he had helped beat Smith, but there was no one to thank him for it. He was an implacable foe, and yet he was capable of kind deeds even to his enemies. He was skeptical of the germ theory of disease, but pain and death moved him deeply.

To New York, which to his mind combined the most disreputable features of both Sodom and Gomorrah, he must remain as the greatest pulpit reformer of the age. If he had lived until 1933 he might have observed a few hopeful signs. He would have seen hungry people who once had plenty, ragged people who once wore good clothes, men broken in spirit who once were vain and haughty—all these he would have seen coming back into the churches. True, most of the churches themselves were impoverished, but the prodigal sons were coming back. Straton would have liked that.

In 1933 even Bishop Manning's great Cathedral of

St. John the Divine had felt the pinch of hard times,
and the Bishop had a conference with the leaders of
the building trades who besought him to resume work
on the building of the great pile which was to be "a
house of prayer for all people." The men wanted
work. And the Bishop told them he would be glad to
put hundreds, even thousands, to work, but where
was the money?

In 1932, when the pinch of economic distress was
at its worst, nearly a million Americans went back to
the church. Although the churches were without the
funds of boom times, when a handful of wealthy
parishioners could do big things, most of them were
able to pay their own way, after making drastic re-
trenchments. Of course it must be borne in mind
that church buildings are exempt from taxation and
would still stand as places of worship even if no one
contributed a cent to their upkeep. Even the buildings that are mortgaged are relatively safe from foreclosure.

During the year the Baptists (this, too, would have
pleased Straton, provided not too many of them were
of the Modernist persuasion) led the Protestant de-
nominations with an increase of 347,353. In New
York City the population is divided fairly evenly into
three groups: Catholics, Jews, and all the rest, including Protestants.

The man who knows most about the relation of

good times to church membership is Dr. Herman C. Weber, statistician of the General Council of the Presbyterian Church. He uses methods in charting religious trends which are similar to the methods used by Roger W. Babson in plotting business cycles. He finds that the graphs bear out the assumption that luxury and indulgence are not conducive to church membership. "Another suggestion," he points out, "is that the so-called good business of the last decade had something at its core so irreligious and unsound that its reflection may be found in the loss of faith in religion."

However much the economic breakdown may strengthen the membership rolls of the churches, it is certain that evangelism will have very little to do with it. New York always has been notoriously deaf to evangelical appeal, and indications are that it becomes steadily more so. Straton was the last of the better known of the city's clergymen even to attempt it. The man who perhaps most closely resembles Straton in his liking for publicity is Dr. Reisner, the Methodist, and he does not rely upon evangelical appeal. Instead he follows a fairly safe middle course, criticizing drinking, swearing, dirty literature, gambling, risqué plays, divorces and all the other obvious frailties of the human race. But he is very cheerful about it all, and never has recourse to the fire and brimstone school of exhortation.

In all truth, New York would be a hard town to save, and most of the pastors, realizing this, go about their business quietly, hoping that they can put down internal dissension and keep their budgets balanced. In the old days it was different; indeed, Jonathan Edwards in 1735 reported that he had "saved" every man, woman and child in Northampton, Mass. He couldn't do that in the New York of today.

The cost of making converts in the foreign mission field, what with the overhead, salaries to missionaries and other expenses, comes to about $260 a head, whereas the average for the United States is about $450 a head. In wicked New York the average cost of making a convert is placed by the most optimistic statistician at $660, and other experts who have tried to figure it out say that $1,500 would be more nearly the correct figure. Many New Yorkers regard this as an outrageously high price to pay, even for an immortal soul, and suspect that it may even be bad business, as the dangers of backsliding in New York are perhaps greater than in any other city in the country.

The fight has been long, slow and discouraging to the preachers. The first Methodist Church in America was set up in New York City. Mrs. Barbara Heck discovered her brother, Paul Runckle, playing cards in a hayloft in John Street, New York, and was much upset. She upbraided him, burned his cards and sent to England for her cousin, Philip Embury, who came over and organized a church. In John Street there still is a Methodist Church, but on that same street, and the streets nearby in lower Manhattan, the research worker today may find also a great many other things which would have shocked Barbara— Wall Street speculators buying jewelry for their sweeties, young men and old patronizing the gin-mills, speakeasies and malt and hop stores of the neighborhood, street gamins shooting dice on the side-walk and hoping to grow up into Big Shots like Nick the Greek, and many other evidences of sin and loose-ness of sorts which have been the worry of reformers since the beginnings of history.

Most of the clergy realize this, as they realize the futility of railing about it, and so they attend to their duties with little fanfare. This is especially true of the Catholics, who control virtually all of the town's political life and most of whatever morals may be found there. Only rarely does a clergyman, unless he is an out-and-out sensationalist or a visiting evangelist out to make a name for himself, revert to the ranting type of preaching which is still in vogue in many parts of America. Few reach the eloquent bitterness of Straton, who once described the women of New York in the words of Juvenal, "lewd, drunken, reel-ing ripe with wine."

Patrick Cardinal Hayes, for the Catholics, sticks to the old faith, with now and then a word against immodest dress, foul literature, divorce and birth control; such Jews as Rabbi Stephen S. Wise and Dr. Nathan Krass plead with the young to defend the ancient beliefs of an ancient race; Bishop Manning of the Episcopalians, busy with his cathedral, usually is all business. And Dr. Reisner, happy, regrets that there are one million young people in the city who have had no more religious education than if they had grown up in Africa. John Haynes Holmes, the brilliant free-lance, breaks most of his lances with politicians whom he regards as corrupt or unsound, but he gets almost nowhere. Straton was the only one who would fight—and the city laughed at him.

THE BAD EARTH

BROADWAY, unlike Greenwich Village, is not a
state of mind but a peculiarly excited condition
of fourth-rate emotions. It is a long and
crooked street, and once, so say the iconographers, it
was a cowpath. Now it is cantharides to cheap souls.

By day it is drab to the point of being revolting; by
night it is loud and garish, the end-product of the fine
lighting trick that Thomas Alva Edison stole from the
gods. It is the capital of America's amusement world.
Other towns have their Main Stems, which at bottom
are the same as Broadway, but Broadway remains the
Mecca of the plaintive crooner, the moony song
writer, the girl whose thighs have been spoken of fa-
vorably, the hoofer who laid 'em in the aisles in
Arkansas City, and all the rest of that crew of wistful home town boys and girls who seek to overreach
themselves.

Broadway is a street of synthetic romance, of
phony titillation. To it come the raw materials for
the broken hearts, celebrated in song and saga, and
for the crushed butterflies, whose singed wings are
Exhibit A in many a smelly scandal.

Ah, what loves the street evokes! And what fun!
What characters, who entwine themselves with hoops

of asafetida around the heartstrings! Good old Shubert Brothers! Good old Larry Fay, now a-moldering in his grave! Dear Nicky Arnstein, so careful with the body God gave him! Dear Harold Russell Ryder! Sweet Vivian Gordon, brainiest of kept women! Dear Minskys, who brought burlesque uptown! Dear lovable, misunderstood Arnold Rothstein! Dear phonies, gyps, fakers, pitchmen and con artists! Dear—but enough of this. The street gets you.

Steadily, insistently, the place has gone honkytonk. Coney Island, saddest of all so-called amusement centers, has moved into the Broadway of Diamond Jim Brady, of George M. Cohan and of James B. Regan. Mr. Cohan once loved the place, for he is of Broadway, and he wrote "Forty-five Minutes from Broadway," "Broadway Jones" and "Hello, Broadway." After a tour of the 1933 Broadway Mr. Cohan composed this off-hand:

"It means the increase in honky-tonk joints,
   The blast of the radios from the amplifiers hanging
      over dance-hall doorways,
   The pedlers and the barkers shouting at the top of
      their lungs:
   'Buy a balloon an' act natural';
   'Come in and see the great flea circus';
   'This way for a good time, folks';
   'No tights in this show';

'Plenty of seats in the first balcony; "She Kissed Him
   to Death" just starting';
'Magnificent love story; bring the children.' "

It is even worse than that.   Once a street of com-
paratively modest tastes, of some show of decorum, it
has degenerated into something resembling the main
drag of a frontier town.   Once there were lobster
palaces and cabarets; now it is cut-rate.   From Forty-
second to Fifty-seventh Street Times Square in 1933
had seventeen dance-halls, with prices ranging from
one cent to five cents a dance, "with 200 most beautiful hostesses as your dancing partners."
   An old army sergeant, aided by fast-spieling salesmen, lectures on health soap, psyllium seeds and re-
ducing belts, with dire threats of the toxic poisoning
habit.   Another lecturer, armed with vials filled with
chemicals of many colors, pleads for the buying of
real estate near the Muscle Shoals development in
Alabama.   The old Chinatown buses are still there,
with their women decoys, or "shills."   Another up
and coming creature offers "Ten Recitations for Ten
Cents," among the ten being the celebrated "Down
in the Lehigh Valley."   Haberdasheries are closing out
at reduced prices; a fire sale is going full blast; an auction sale of fantastic gewgaws draws enough people to
block the sidewalk; a pushcart pedler exhibits "100
per cent pure whisky candies—three for five cents."

Below Forty-second Street the garment trades, with their workers who pour out of the tall buildings and place a blight on the streets like so many ravening grasshoppers, have steadily inched their way northward. It became so bad, indeed, that when Grover A. Whalen was Police Commissioner he set aside one block between Seventh and Eighth avenues as a sort of "play street" for these doubtless well-intentioned but ungraceful people to pass their moments of relaxation. It didn't do a great deal of good.

The police, backed by ordinances a mile long, have tried at times to restore the street, in its more horrendous reaches, to something like ordinary respectability and comfort. They have arrested pushcart pedlers, sidewalk obstructionists, noise-makers and other nuisances by the drove, but it has done little good. The Magistrates, notorious for their deep human sympathy, usually discharge the prisoners, who rush right back to resume their business of trying to sell things to people that the people don't want.

The decline of the old street, where, they tell us, giants once walked, may be blamed upon several causes—the growth of radio and the motion picture, the depression of 1929 which forced restaurants and all other types of retail business in that area to trim their prices, and the awful decline in real estate values, which was not helped by the building of the great Rockefeller Center project between Fifth and Sixth

avenues.   Perhaps, also, there has been a continued
downward trend in the public taste, although the students of social trends seem pretty sure that the American is becoming more and more sophisticated, and
better educated, more appreciative of the sound
things of life, as time goes on.

Whatever the reason, or combination of reasons,
Broadway has become a basement bargain counter.
It has places where one may go, with no cover charge,
and gorge on cheap food while watching a ridiculous
floor show.   Bus terminals, with their lumbering,
smelly vehicles, had edged their way into the choice
spots, offering transportation at less than the rail-
roads.   In the summer a stand is a breakaway soft
drink place; in the winter it is a nuttery.   There are
chow-meineries, peep shows for men only, flea cir-
cuses, lectures on what killed Rudolph Valentino, jit-
ney ballrooms and a farrago of other attractions
which would have sickened the heart of the Broad-
wayite of the period of even ten years ago.

Legal 3.2% beer hasn't helped the tone much.   Indeed, it has angered the coffee shops and the soft drink
places.   The money-makers are the larger places,
where as many people as possible may be taken care
of with the greatest possible speed, whether it is a
dance hall or "the longest bar in the world."   The
tempo, never too smooth and sedate at best, grows
daily cheaper and uglier.   At the Montmartre, where

once the town's swells and their out of town friends were glad to pay a $5 cover charge, has opened to take care of the strange people who go to dance for five cents a dance.

The side streets running off Broadway are not much better than the old Street of Broken Hearts itself. These side streets, for the most part, take their tone from the Main Stem, although one may still find excellent restaurants, sound speakeasies, and a few fairly good retail shops only a few doors away.

The trend to cheapness on the side streets has been inevitable. Take the case of the old Keen's Chop House in Forty-fourth Street between Broadway and Sixth Avenue, which was a good place to eat for a few years after prohibition. Then it declined, fell into the hands of William Duffy, prize-fight manager and dear old pal of the underworld, who kept it for a time as a wide-open barroom and restaurant. He finally gave up and the place gathered cobwebs until Bernarr Macfadden took it over as one of his penny restaurants, where a derelict just this side of starvation may get something known as food for as little as one cent.

All this, to be sure, is not to argue that Mr. Macfadden's enterprise is not in every way as worthy as Mr. Duffy's whisky and chop tavern, or the earlier Keen's, where actors came in to eat their chops and steaks with a dash of Major Gray's chutney. Mr.

few property owners who would like to change the street are powerless; they don't want to go broke.

The street, its people and its character, resemble something conceived by those *entrepreneurs* of burlesque, the Minskys. The Minskys are, and were, a great family. There were four brothers, Abraham, Billy, Herbert and Morton, and of the four, Billy, now dead, was the greatest. Once the first citizens of East Houston Street, they moved their burlesque shows to Broadway and carried on the tradition of heavy buttocks and heavier jokes.

Originally the idea of the old burlesque house, the Winter Garden on the East Side, was to cater to low tastes in a low section. Billy Minsky improved this, and when he moved uptown he decreed that not all the girls had to weigh more than 170 pounds. Not every comedian had to have a red nose and clout his stooge in the pants with a bludgeon. He wanted speed, a dash of smartness, and a trace of what was known as Broadway style. Tex Rickard, at his prizefights, used to worship the top hats. It meant that nice people were coming to his shows. The Minskys, when their East Side burlesque house began to hit the popular consciousness, felt the same way about it.

In his uptown houses, Billy, with a brain that reeked with ideas, wanted to try out his philosophy of burlesque. He said: "Broad burlesque and satire even flavor our contemporary dramas and comedies." He

Macfadden may have the right idea. But ton

The change in Broadway's fine old flavor
come overnight. Indeed, some hard-bitten ge
who have stuck to the street through the
argue that the first visible sign of degenerati
along about 1912, when the East Side stuss
from whom were drawn such men as the n
Herman Rosenthal, began moving uptown
were drawn by the irresistible urge to be am
people; they found a few nice people there t
there aren't many left.

The faces of the people themselves seem ur
freaks come to life from a dreadful nightm
some noon in the hunting-room restaurant o
tor, by the window, and look down at the :
figures. There will pass the most astoun
gregation—cauliflower ears, beggars, sleaz)
skinny girls who would be out of place in
cheapest dance hall, twisted old men, slee
with pale faces, the blind and the maime
have reached Broadway, where the hopef
from a thousand towns long to be.

Cheap dances, lewd burlesque, filthy pic
the hallmarks of the New Broadway. N
shoutings of the reformers, not all the pious
the police, can do anything about it, for th
fill what appears to be a genuine human n

had a new show each week. The title of one was "Ima Pansy from Central Park," and of another, "Ada Onion from Bermuda." Bill started a sidewalk cooch show to drag in the customers. It was all pretty raw; the police didn't like it, and neither did the censors or the members of the Forty-second Street Association. Billy eased up a bit, and to counteract the depression he made his jokes a bit more anatomical and stripped his girls a little closer to the ham bone. He died in 1932 while in the midst of wrangles with the authorities.

The rest of the family and their partners, after many quarrels over business matters and questions of taste, continue to supply New York with burlesque. The basis of burlesque is not greatly different from the theme of more than one high-toned popular stage play, but the girls are not as pretty, the lines are not as broad and the boob-fetching tease is not so obvious. Although missing the inspired touch of Billy Minsky, the shows are sure to continue to have an appeal for customers who wish to experience a certain sort of low belly laugh.

The dance-hall, too, must continue to thrive, for almost as far back as the Founding Fathers this institution has been deemed to fill a definite human need. And always it has been an outlaw among amusements. It is neither night club nor saloon. It is neither altogether nice nor altogether disreputable. Some sound

thinkers have defended it; others, especially the reformers, have either tried to kill it or to wash its face
until it would be beyond recognition.

The Strand Roof was founded originally by some
exceptionally high-minded ladies so that working
girls, seeking innocent relaxation after hours, might
have a place where they could dance innocently under
the stars.   Others had the same avowed purpose, and
in most of them, in a short time, it was found that
there were cadets, procurers and other types of loaf-
ers.   In essence, the dance-hall is a place for social
misfits, including lonely hearts.   In the closed halls,
where men only are admitted to dance with the
hostesses, one may encounter a peculiar type of seedy
individual who is a constant customer and who finds
all his life's pleasure wholly in the hall.

Reformers and preachers always have insisted that
the dance-halls are places where girls are ruined, and
that the hostesses all live in sin, or worse.   This is not
always true.   More often than not the girls are merely
honest working girls, who like to dance and have fun.
In one dance-hall twenty-two girls in one year trotted
with 52,221 men at the rate of thirty-five cents for
each three dances.   That was before the depression.
By 1933 many halls charged one cent a dance.

The lower type of dance-hall, the closed joint, is a
direct lineal descendant of the old mining camp dive.
Its main purpose is to give the unattractive man a

chance to have a good time. And how unattractive
some of them are! Some of the old sourdoughs could
pass for Apollos beside them. To these places come
the crippled, the outcasts, the pockmarked, and frequently Filipinos, who are extremely fond of the
dance. Curiously, the police say that the foreigners
are usually much better behaved than the loutish na-
tive American, who usually goes to such places, not
for artistic reasons, but in the hope of picking up a
girl.

In New York each dance-hall must be licensed; the
police, in theory at least, also keep watch on them.
The halls continue to be ruled by the fashions of the
times and the moral and esthetic whims of the proprietors. The first rule laid down to the bouncer is
to keep the place clean, but not too clean. Spitting
on the floor is a practise usually frowned upon.
Leaving empty booze flasks on the floor is not tolerated in the better joints. One girl was rebuked for
carrying a knife, or frog-sticker, in her stocking.
Many places for a while let their girls take off their
dresses and cavort in their rompers on special nights,
but the License Commissioner didn't approve, though
sometimes the rompers came below the knees. Fantastic postures, such as the Strangler Lewis hold
around the neck, are barred from the more tony
palaces.

Connoisseurs of such matters say that Chicago,

Philadelphia, Boston, St. Louis and Kansas City, in particular, have excellent dance-halls, but that the girls in those cities are not quite as intelligent as the New York girls. Their conversation, for one thing, is not as sparkling, and many of them chew gum.

It is, however, from the dance-halls, from the lower type of night club (which is a sort of cheap speak-easy and miniature dance-hall combined) and from the thug-operated barrooms that much delinquency, vice and crime arise. And yet, even the reformers have ceased to hope that dance-halls can be wiped out. They may not understand precisely why they fill a social need, but they sense it dimly.

Even the better hotels in the White Light District, which have managed to keep open, show the signs of the cheapening of the district. They offer meals on the roof at low prices. They cater to people who would hardly have been allowed inside a dining-room of any good hotel ten years ago. There is the story of the wealthy gambler who owned an apartment hotel just off Broadway. He ran into a newspaper man while walking down the street one day and invited him to move into the hotel, take the best apartment and live there rent free.

"I couldn't do that," said the newspaper man. "I might take an apartment there, but I'd want to pay you for it."

The gambler begged.

"Why are you so damned insistent?" asked the newspaper man.

"Well, I'll tell you. I want it to be a nice place. Nobody lives there now except me, some gunmen, kept women, bootleggers, crapshooters, confidence men and dope pedlers. You have two small children. I figure that if you moved in and put a baby carriage outside, maybe some nice people would want to live there."

During the whole prohibition period there were few really good speakeasies in what could be strictly called the Broadway sector. For a good drink, usually, a thirsty man would be forced to go to a regular restaurant where he knew the proprietor, or he would have to go out of his way two or three blocks. This shameful condition may be traced directly to the inability of Broadway to conduct any enterprise on a high level of character. "The liquor is rotten, but it's an easy place to get to," was the verdict of Broadway drinkers on the status of their own speakeasies. Thus the high-hat drinkers, who were willing to go as much as $1 for a drink, moved their trace to the section east of Broadway, principally in the Fifties.

Moreover, neither the police nor the Federal agents wanted speakeasies to operate too brazenly on Broadway proper. Let them move to a side street. For a time the Federal men said that Forty-fifth Street was the wettest street in the country. One bar on Forty-

fourth Street was raided forty times in five years; no
one could find the owner and no one could prove who
operated it.   In anger, the Federals finally padlocked
it, anyhow.

One man got into trouble with the authorities, who
said he did not have the proper credentials to operate
a cabaret or night club.   His defense, which was successful, was that his joint was neither a night club nor
a cabaret, but only a cheap speakeasy with a five-cent
piano.

Another man, proprietor of a low speakeasy just off
Broadway, called the police one night and asked them
to remove the body of a man who had just died there.
"He didn't get it in here," the boss explained to the
police, who removed the body after examining seventeen quarts of "good stuff" back of the bar.

Nevertheless, for all its lack of dignity, the small
speakeasy, which had a small bar and sometimes a few
tables, was essentially a Broadway institution.   Like
Broadway itself, there was nothing quite like it in
most other cities.   The worst city in the country in
which to obtain a drink of good liquor during the
prohibition era was Washington, D. C.   Men from
Broadway, ingenious, alert, with beagle noses for
whisky, have searched Washington for hours without
finding anything except corn whisky or inferior
Maryland rye.   It is far from idle fancy to suggest
that if only one-tenth of the smaller New York

speakeasies could have been moved to Washington, proprietors and all, and allowed to operate without molestation, half the horrors of the Coolidge and Hoover administrations could have been banished, or at least vastly ameliorated.

From the joint which ran under Broadway just above City Hall, to the skyscraper roof-speakeasy in the Fifties, Manhattan Island had them to spare. How many were there? The estimates range from the 100,000 of the more optimistic down to the mere 800, which was the figure set by one of the few New York prohibitionists in the boom year of 1926. In the spring of 1933, just before the coming of 3.2% beer, the secret estimate of the New York police placed the figure at 9,000, which included cordial shops and all other places known to sell liquor. Probably the police did not find all the places; certainly, according to their own estimates, this figure was much lower than in the boom years.

For economic reasons, it was found that New York could support a handful of luxurious speakeasies and a great number of the dirtier, darker, unadorned places. The big place, with its Babylonian gardens and costly mirrors, might make money for a time, but unless protection was sure, it was a safe bet that sooner or later it would be wrecked. The police under Whalen, and the hatchet Federals under Maurice

Campbell, wrecked many a noble barroom under the public nuisance law.

Whalen's drive, which closed up a few places permanently and many others for several hours, was directed chiefly at places which sold impure liquor. He made his raids on the basis of chemical reports showing the sale of bad liquor, but upon examination it was found that most of this booze, though not fit for the old Waldorf bar, was not much more dangerous to health, if taken in moderation, than the bulk of the so-called good stuff being sold. For example, the highest percentage of wood alcohol found in any of the samples was one-half of one per cent—not a pleasant thought, but far from fatal.

It is to the credit of most of the speakeasy proprietors that they tried to sell as good stuff as they could obtain. The worst that could be said against most of it was that it had been cut too much—or "Gilletted," as the saying had it.

The other side of the picture, the sinister side, was horrible in its reality. A few places, from time to time, were caught selling a varnish-like concoction, compounded mostly of wood alcohol, which would send the victims reeling, blind or dying into the street. From the beginning of prohibition the alcoholic ward of Bellevue Hospital, which is the surest barometer of the devastating drinking habits of the city, showed a steady increase in the number of admissions.

The link which some speakeasy owners had with known criminals led to many a messy situation, distinctly embarrassing to all concerned. The worst thing, for prestige particularly, is to have a serious fight or a killing in a joint. One of the most celebrated cases was at the Club Abbey in West Fifty-fourth Street. It was a pleasant early morning in January. Earlier in the evening Larry Fay, the racketeer, had been in, but had left with a party of friends to attend the Beaux Arts Ball and mingle with the bon ton. Among those known to have been present at this late hour were Arthur Flegenheimer, more commonly known as Dutch Schultz, the Bronx beer baron; Charles Sherman, racketeer and friend of Arnold Rothstein who at that time was under indictment for murder in Massachusetts; a man of the white lights surnamed Crumpet, but usually known simply as Marty the Wolf, and a member of New York's "Finest," Detective John J. Walsh, who was sitting in the "cuff" or "red ink" corner, a spot reserved for accomplished gangsters, representatives of the law, and a few Broadway columnists who don't feel they should be called upon to pay for their food, drink and entertainment.

How the trouble started is a moot point, and Detective Walsh later insisted that he had left before hostilities became serious, but the best version is that the Wolf was dancing with a girl. Sherman was sit-

ting alone, brooding.   Schultz was drunk.   Every
now and then Sherman would get up and whisper
something to Schultz.   Suddenly, as the saying has it,
everything went black.   The club was reduced to a
shambles.   Tables were broken, the walls peppered
with shots, and several dents in the floor indicated
that skulls might have landed there.   When it was all
over Miss Mavis King, Broadway's most beautiful cigarette girl, took Sherman to Polyclinic Hospital.   He
had been shot and he bore ten stab wounds.   He said
nothing.   The police never were able to get at the
bottom of the affair, which probably was a private
quarrel in which at least eight gangsters participated.
About all that happened was that the Club Abbey
soon went out of existence.

Then there was the affair in Porky Murray's speakeasy in West Fifty-second street, near the Guild and
Alvin theaters, late one night in February, 1933.   It
was 2:30 A.M.   John Sweeney, a middle-aged news-
boy, came in with his bundle of papers.   He had just
had a row with a customer who had blacked both his
eyes and he was mumbling to himself.   He called
"Papers" and there was no answer.

Sweeney looked around.   A man and a woman, obviously dead, lay on the floor.   Eight glasses on the
bar and behind it were smashed.   In front of the mirror a little cat was making foolish passes at its reflection.   Sweeney ran out and got Patrolman Abraham

Goldstein.   The policeman looked behind the bar.
Another dead man lay there.

The three dead were identified as John Egan, alias
Doyle and White, a criminal for fifteen years, who
had escaped two months earlier from Warden Lawes's
new and supposedly escape-proof wing at Sing Sing
Prison; Dorothy Miller, alias McCarthy, alias Han-
non, who had once served a term in Bedford Reformatory and who later distinguished herself by throwing
a salt-cellar through a Ninth avenue restaurant window, and Patsy Griffin, once a porter in the speakeasy,
who recently had been promoted to bartender, a job
which he greatly liked.

It seems that Egan and the woman had been talking at the bar, with Patsy Griffin serving drinks, when
one or more men came in.   One of these called Egan
to a corner and a loud quarrel began.   Griffin asked
for quiet and the stranger told him to shut up.   Griffin started for the stranger with a stick which he used
to pack ice.   There was a shot, and Egan fell to the
floor dead, his fully loaded revolver half-way drawn.
The woman turned in time to see Egan fall, and the
stranger pumped several shots into her.   The unfortunate Patsy Griffin, who had seen too much for his
own good, ducked behind the bar, where the stranger
sealed his lips forever.   The murderer never was
found.   Porky Murray, who used to be a Gaelic foot-

ball enthusiast, was extremely sorry about the affair, and paid Patsy Griffin's funeral expenses.

A senseless, pointless business. The wonder is that there were not more killings in similar unexplained circumstances. Efficient bouncers doubtless saved many lives, and the proverbial immunity of drunken men to serious harm, which probably is largely myth, may be held responsible for saving others.

The worst creature, of all the army of parasites who carried on their trade along Broadway during the speakeasy period, was the proprietor of the "clip joint." Ever since the beginnings of Manhattan Island there have been resorts where it was not safe for a man to go unless he sought to be beaten up, drugged, or robbed, or all three. There are not a great many of these places, but the few which have been discovered are enough. The clip joint preys on the New Yorker and the out of town sport alike.

A crooked taxicab driver usually makes a suggestion to a likely looking passenger that he can take him to a place where he can "have a good time." Many men who ought to know better, indeed, men who regard themselves in their own modest way as wise guys, able to take care of themselves in any emergency, have accepted such an invitation. Inside the place, they drink themselves into a stupor, usually talking to some of the girls who are a part of the staff of the place, and then, finally, the time comes to pay the bill.

Well, suppose the bill, outrageously high, comes to more than the customer thinks he owes. Of what use is argument, with at least four rough-looking customers leering on? Very well. He will pay. But he hasn't enough cash. The proprietor agrees to take a check. He examines the signature, pronounces it indistinct, pretends to tear up the check and asks the customer to try again. In this fashion the clip joint proprietor may get several checks. In addition, he may say, "Never mind the checks. I'll tear 'em up. We know you're all right. Just give us an I O U and we can collect any time."

The next day, if the victim checks with his bank, he will find that he has been rooked. Moreover, a horribly hard-looking customer will likely as not call at his office to get cash for the I O U. Then comes remorse, anger and terror. Usually they pay, but not always. The sensible ones call the police, who, be it said to their credit, are death on "clip joints" when they have a definite complaint.

Achille Mirner, a jeweler, was beaten to death in a "clip joint" when he protested that he was being robbed. His murderers went to prison. Many of the joints have been raided and wrecked. Often it is difficult to convict the operators of these abbatoirs, for the victim, even when he can identify the place and the people who robbed him, often fears that his family will hear about it, or, even worse, that he will appear silly before his friends. Recently a wealthy man from the South, stopping at the Waldorf-Astoria, was gypped of almost $2,000 one night, and a grim visitor the next morning was asking for another $1,000 on an I O U. He got in touch with a friend, who told him to tell the collector to go to hell, and that the police would be there soon. The Confederate visitor didn't have enough nerve to go through with it. He told the collector to come back in an hour. Then, in an utter panic, he checked up and took the next train out of New York.

Raiding a clip joint is one of the most exhilarating experiences which can befall anyone. The police, even those who are not sadists at heart, throw all abandon aside when they are on such an errand. To the privileged witness, the wrecking of the joint is as pleasantly exciting as having a ringside seat at one of the decisive battles of history. The plot works like this:

One morning at 11 o'clock the telephone rang in a newspaper office. It was a call for one of the editors, from a friend of his, a lawyer who lived in a hotel on Fifth avenue in the Fifties. The lawyer was shouting in rage. He explained that, at breakfast time that morning, he had been disturbed by a scratching and fumbling at the door. He opened it and in fell a kinsman of his, a young man just out of college. The youngster, a strapping athlete, was groggy and bleeding. He mumbled a story of having been robbed in a joint, of being tortured and tied by the wrists, which were red and swollen.

"What can be done about it?" asked the lawyer.

"Can the young man find the place, and will he guide the police to it and go through with the complaint?"

"Yes," said the lawyer. The newspaper man got in touch with the police, and that night at 9 o'clock two of the best men from Headquarters sat down beside the youth's bed in the hotel and got from him all he remembered of his adventures. He had fallen for the invitation of a taxicab driver. He wasn't quite sure where he had been. He thought he could find it. Yes, there had been some women, and they had come to his table and talked and drunk with him. He remembered dimly that they hadn't seemed very attractive. He recalled that, with one last attempt at caution, he had tried to hide some of his money in his shoe, but they had got that money too. And there had been checks. He wasn't sure how many he had signed, or for what amounts.

One of the detectives shook his head. "It's a long chance," he said. "I don't think he can find it. They rarely remember where they were. I wish they did. We'd wreck 'em all."

It was decided to start the bloody safari at 3 o'clock in the morning, that being the hour when the vultures are in full feather. The detectives told the boy to try to sleep, and then they went down, got into a police car with two other detectives, and went off to see a friend, who passed the time with them until half an hour before the time set for the search for the enemy. A detective telephoned the young man, who got out of bed, caught a taxicab and joined the raiding group. All piled into the police car.

They cruised slowly through the West Side streets. Several times the victim almost recognized a familiar façade, and then shook his head. Finally he said: "Stop the car. It's along here somewhere. Let me out a minute." He got out, looked up and down the street, and then pointed to a brownstone basement. "That's the place," he said.

The detectives rang the doorbell. The door opened. Four ratty-looking young men sprang up. "Are these the men?" asked the leader of the raiding squad. "I recognize two of them," said the victim. There was a show of resistance, as the police euphemism puts it, and inside of a minute the four men found in the resort were writhing on the floor, groaning and begging for mercy. Badly beaten by the detectives, who did all of it with their fists and legs, the four were lined up against the wall. While one detective questioned them, the other three began a thorough, systematic wrecking of the joint.

The bar was pulled up by its roots and broken. Every table and chair was splintered. Even the bottles and the glasses were smashed. There were horrendous sounds as the big mirrors crashed. Draperies and chandeliers were pulled down with a deafening clatter. Within half an hour the clip joint looked like one of those old pictures of devastated Belgium. The prisoners were carted off to jail, and the young man who had been robbed the night before went back to his hotel to bed.

Of course, it might be pointed out that the young man had no business listening to the siren song of a plug-ugly cab driver. He might have had more sense. Doubtless he has more sense now. But the number of suckers who are ripe for plucking by the Broadway crows, although never computed by census, must be enormous, even infinite. And for every man who is ready to get himself into a jam, there are ten waiting to help him.

There aren't many clip joints, but Broadway is the clip street of the world, the slaughter house of Moronia.

SOME PIGS AND WHISTLES

I. JIMMY WALKER, THE DREAM PRINCE

"A REFORMER is a guy who rides through a sewer in a glass-bottomed boat."—From the sayings of former Mayor James J. Walker of New York.

The great James was the paradox of American politics. He was esteemed as a wit; his favorite humorist was Arthur (Bugs) Baer. He was called the best-dressed man in public life; actually his clothes were ultra-Broadwayish, in highly questionable taste according to Racquet and Tennis Club standards, and designed principally to keep him from looking as skinny as he was. He was accounted a public speaker with a gift for clear statement; a transcript of any of his extemporaneous speeches will show that many of his sentences don't parse (this is a curious weakness possessed also by that overrated orator, William Jennings Bryan, whose sentences, as spoken, sometimes trailed off into nothingness).

He could, on occasion, put on a solemn face and be as dignified as Buddha; on other occasions he could, in high glee, get down on the floor and roll the dice with the boys, for he loved African golf with a Beale street fervor. His favorite tear-jerker, in his speeches, was a declaration of his great affection for New York City, the magnificent metropolis where he was born; when hard times were pressing, he raised salaries, and plunged his beloved city into a financial mess from which it may not be extricated for a generation.

He was supposed to be glib, and quick-witted, as on the famous day when, in the Legislature, he killed the so-called Clean Books Bill with the observation, "I never heard of a man or a woman who was ruined by a book"; summoned before Governor Roosevelt to answer charges, he didn't make sense, among his answers being, "If it is wrong, it is unethical." He always insisted that he was open, forthright, aboveboard and all that sort of thing; he used the phrase "off the record" to handcuff his newspaper questioners more than any man who ever held public office.

He spoke at Holy Name breakfasts, and always had a good word for his Church, which was the Catholic; at the funeral of Marty McCue at St. Patrick's Monsignor John P. Chidwick's praise of the dead man was interpreted as an almost cruelly pointed criticism of the private life of James J. Walker. Alfred E. Smith made him Mayor in the campaign of 1925 to succeed Hearst's marionette, John F. Hylan, and Walker fought for Smith for President at the Chicago convention in 1932 that nominated Roosevelt;

actually Smith and Walker hated each other, for their whole patterns of life and thought were different.

Walker, as the old prizefight managers say of goofy and unmanageable geniuses of the ring, could have been as good as he wanted to be. When he was attending to business, and his attention held for a time to serious matters, he won the admiration of the most hard-headed of New York's bankers and business men by the clarity of his thought and the apparent honesty of his approach. He could see through a tangled situation instantly. If he had wanted to study, he could have led the class.

Sometimes he drank too much, and felt bad the next day. There were days when he wouldn't go to City Hall. At other times he was deathly ill, for he was a frail fellow, and his nerves were pitched in a high key. Always he was boxing with buzz-saws and phantoms, and thinking he could smile off the hurts. He held what probably is the most difficult and complicated administrative job on earth, and if that was not enough to worry him, he had plenty of other things—his own carefree inclinations, his deadly inability to say "no," his bills and his friends, his lack of sleep and rest, and the suspicion, which must have come to him, that the harpies of Tammany would be with him just so long and then they would turn and tear the flesh from his little bones.

Jimmy was a symbol of release to millions of strap-

hangers, and they loved him. Even after he had been
out of office almost a year, and was sunning himself in
the south of France, little groups of New Yorkers
would get together and tell each other that Jimmy
could come back and sweep the city. Napoleon, back
from Elba, would have seemed as nothing. Wrong?
Perhaps, but that's the way many persons felt about
him.

Was he seen with Betty Compton at prizefights on
nights when his wife was either at their home in St.
Luke's place or in Florida? Very well. Good for
Jimmy. Many a man would rather be at a prizefight
with a woman other than his wife.

Did he quit the Mayor's office under fire, in the fact
of almost certain removal by Governor Roosevelt?
Certainly he did. But he was charming anyway, and
a poll of the streets of New York a week after his
resignation showed that all sorts of people would vote
for him again.

Did he trample the tenets of his faith and strike at
the foundations, by his flagrant personal conduct, of
the sacred American home? Yes, yes. But most of
the women of New York, even though they may only
have seen his pictures, loved him and thought that
this saucy-faced, boyish-looking little man should be
allowed to do as he pleased.

Did he take too many long vacations, and let the
business of the city drift along, or be attended to by

incompetents and worse? Of course, but he seemed, for a long time, able to stop all rising criticism by one serious speech or by some spectacular move or crisp aphorism.

He was, for many dizzy, splendiferous years, immune to the more serious forms of criticism which, in other times, would have ruined any man in public life. Father Knickerbocker, his pockets full of new money and his innards full of night club champagne, was more than tolerant to Jimmy. At dinners, parades, luncheons and rallies the band played his old song, "Will You Love Me in December as You Do in May?" which Jimmy had written as a young man, and then Jimmy, the Spirit of New York, would appear to charm the crowd.

Jimmy was of New York, and to the country he typified its gaudiness, smartness and insouciance to perfection. He was born on June 19, 1881, in Leroy Street, Greenwich Village, the son of William H. Walker, a lumber dealer and local political power who had been born in Ireland. Jimmy went to St. Francis Xavier and then to New York Law School for three years. He fiddled around with song writing, banking, promotion schemes and what not, and decided to enter politics. He was elected to the State Assembly in 1909, and served there under the wing of Alfred E. Smith, who already had been in the Assembly for eight terms. In 1911, in an estimate of the members of the Legislature, appeared this summary of Walker:

"James J. Walker—Lumber; educated St. Francis Xavier; elected to the Assembly in 1909, and reelected last fall; an intelligent and capable man, who devoted his energies to help put through the Tammany legislative program, his chief contribution being through participation in the debates; Citizens Union says that most of his recorded votes were " 'against public interest.' "

Meanwhile Jimmy had passed his bar examinations. He soon developed a fairly good law practise. As a lawyer, he at one time or another represented such diverse interests as a meat-packing company and the killer of the gangster, Kid Dropper. Although far from profound, he knew the ropes, and he was excellent in his courtroom appearance.

In 1914 he went to the State Senate, where he remained, either as minority or majority leader, depending upon whether the Republicans or the Democrats had the upper hand, until, in 1925, he agreed to run in the Democratic primaries against Mayor John F. Hylan. At that time Walker was coming along rapidly. His acquaintance was enormous. He had sided with the element of the so-called "New Tammany," the other members of which were such men as Al Smith, Robert F. Wagner and James A. Foley. This New Tammany, with Walker driving through its

legislation at Albany, was friendly toward social legislation, which was good policy.

Moreover, Jimmy had aligned himself with the lib-
erals, which endeared him to New York City. He
made it possible for the city to have Sunday sports;
he was the father of the boxing law, which was named
after him, and which permitted some of the greatest
and most costly fights in history.

The city was sick of eight years of Hylan. Even
the Citizens Union, that organization of consistent
fault-finders, had a good word for the legislative record and the natural ability of James J. Walker. For
a time he worked hard at City Hall. He said that a
lot of dust had been swept under the sofa and that he
would clean it out. There were days, during the first
splendid months, when he worked at City Hall sixteen hours a day.

After four years of playing, during which there
were little more than whispers of serious derelictions
of duty, he came up for reelection. The Citizens
Union this time criticized his handling of the police,
referred to graft in the Department of Markets, payroll padding in the Department of Street Cleaning,
and questioned the propriety of Mr. Walker's part in
the Equitable bus franchise deal. His Republican op-
ponent, Fiorello H. LaGuardia, attacked Tammany
and Walker all the way down the line. LaGuardia
was on the right track, but he didn't have all his

proofs nailed down, and the people of New York, in those gaudy days, were in no mood for reform. Walker swamped LaGuardia.

It was in his second term that the far-off drums began to roll. There were ominous whisperings. Finally, the Appellate Division began its investigation of the lower courts, and unraveled the tangled, sordid situation under which stool pigeons had framed innocent women, policemen had assaulted and robbed and taken bribes from women of the streets and even honest old householders. It smelled to Heaven.

Then, in 1931, the Legislature, with Samuel Seabury as counsel, began its long, patient inquiry into the government of New York City. The investigating committee drew forth amazing details of incompetence, of graft, of the most fantastic financial operations, but it was a long time before Walker began to fit into the picture—Walker, the man for whom Seabury had been gunning from the first. It was not until April, 1932, that Seabury called Walker to the stand. It was a great fencing match, with Walker, glib and flip as ever, but looking tired around the gills, answering the questions of the plodding old jurist. In June Seabury handed to Governor Roosevelt fifteen conclusions drawn from the testimony, and called Walker unfit to continue in office. In August the Governor held the removal hearings in Albany.

It was at this hearing that Roosevelt demonstrated
a peculiar quality of his mind—his ability to master
the details, and the implications, of an appalling, con-
fusing mass of testimony. When he came to question
Walker he knew exactly what he was doing; apparently he knew ten times as much about the testimony
as Walker, whose virtually sole defense was to impute
political motives to the investigators. It was a fore-
gone conclusion, after his showing before Roosevelt,
that the Governor would have to remove him; Walker
beat the Governor to it by resigning on September 1,
1932.

He said he had been the victim of an unfair trial
and that he would "go to the people" for reelection.
He went abroad, and was hurrying back for the Democratic city convention when his ship was delayed.
He took another ship, and radioed to John F. Curry,
the leader of Tammany, that he would not run.
Curry named Surrogate John O'Brien, a paragon of
all the private virtues, to make the race for the unex-
pired term of Walker. O'Brien was almost everything that Walker was not. He was named in obedience to a sound political law which Walker himself
once put into words when he changed Police Commissioners:

"When you are making up a bill for a vaudeville
show, you don't have two numbers of the same kind
in succession. You wouldn't follow John McCor-

mack with Lawrence Tibbett.   You wouldn't have
one banjo act follow another banjo act."

In semi-disgrace, his pride hurt, not knowing what
friends he had left, harassed by debts, Walker went
back to France and passed the winter there.   He sailed
on the same ship with his old friend, Betty Compton,
the actress, and they were together much of the time
that winter.   In the spring of 1933 Mrs. Janet Allen
Walker, whom Jimmy had married back in the days
when he was a song writer, at a time when Betty was
a baby, obtained a divorce in Florida on the grounds
of desertion.

On April 18 Walker and Betty Compton were
married at Cannes, France.   They traveled over Europe.   Walker worked for Hearst for a short time during the World Economic Conference in London, sending back reports to the Hearst papers.   Reports came
back that he was happy, without a grievance against
anyone, even Roosevelt.   His latest wisecrack was
when someone in France told him of a new Italian
liner that had stabilizers.   "I wish I had a pair for
Tammany," he said.

New York remembers him with a sneaking affection mingled with contempt that a man of such gifts
should have allowed himself to become hopelessly en-
tangled.   Some say he had salted away enough money
to last him for the rest of his life; others hold that he
was broke when he gave up his $40,000 a year job

as Mayor. Certainly, in letters to his old friends, he has asked them, if they knew of any profitable legal work he could attend to abroad, to let him know. John Curry, the sly, gray old boss of Tammany, was enormously fond of Jimmy.

2. CLAY PIGEON OF THE UNDERWORLD

Jack (Legs) Diamond (born John T. Nolan of Philadelphia) was a frail, tubercular little rat, cunning and cruel. He liked to burn men's feet with matches. He would pour bullets into the bodies of men who lay helpless and dying on the floor. Once he tied a blindfolded man to a tree, put the man's index fingers into the barrels of a shotgun, and went into conference with him on a matter of business.

The police dismissed him as "a cheap little package thief." The master minds of the underworld, particularly the powers who fancied themselves "right guys" and frowned on the torture chamber and assassination, disapproved of Diamond's philosophy of life. He was dangerous and senseless. And yet, the truth is that for a time Diamond was feared above all other New York gunmen; more, for a time he was powerful, and if he had had more executive ability he would have gone far.

He started early in the school of crime along the New York docks. After serving a short term in Leav-

enworth, as a mere kid, for desertion from the Army
and grand larceny, he became one of the most adept
of all the fleet-footed sneak thieves and package
snatchers in New York. His admiring friends called
him "Legs" because of his smooth, quick escapes. He
served a term in the reformatory, but, although arrested many times, he was hard to convict—just as,
later, it seemed almost impossible to kill him.

His first serious experience as a human target was
on an October Sunday in 1924. He was driving up
Fifth avenue. At 110th street some men in another
car opened fire on him. "Legs" was wounded in the
right heel. Other shot peppered his head. He drove
to Mount Sinai Hospital, had himself repaired, and
continued on to his home in the Bronx as if nothing
had happened.

Next came the Sunday evening in October, 1927.
He was pinch-hitting for his brother as bodyguard
for the late Little Augie (Jacob Orgen) and the two
were standing at Norfolk and Delancey streets. An
automobile drove up. There was a terrific barrage of
gunfire. Little Augie died, and they took "Legs" to
Bellevue Hospital, badly wounded in the body. To
the police, who paraded many suspected gunmen past
his bed, Diamond maintained an air of aloof contempt, identifying no one. It was while in the hospital this time that he indulged fully his appetite for

gangster and underworld fiction. His bed was littered with the crime magazines.

The little gunman caught the fancy of Arnold Rothstein, who was always on the alert for promising talent. Rothstein made Diamond his assistant bodyguard, no mean title. After big dice or card games, when some of the boys were afraid to go home with their winnings, Diamond would be assigned to escort them safely. It became the thing at Police Headquarters, when a gambler was found murdered with all his pockets empty, to ask, "Did Legs take him home?"

Diamond's quick temper, and his love for gun play, came very near getting him into trouble in the summer of 1929. He controlled the Hotsy Totsy Club, a hot spot on Broadway. Late one evening Diamond and his partner, Charles Entratta, alias Charles Green, an ex-convict, were serving drinks behind the bar. Three men came in—Simon Walker, an ex-convict; William (Red) Cassidy, and Peter Cassidy, all tough waterfront fighters. The Cassidys got into an argument with the two cobras behind the bar. Diamond and Entratta pulled their guns. Red Cassidy fell with a bullet in his chest and Diamond, leaning over him, emptied his gun into him. Peter Cassidy was badly wounded, but not killed. Simon Walker, who was tough enough but who appears to have been a more or less innocent bystander, was shot and killed by either Diamond or Entratta.

Although there were twenty-five witnesses, no conviction ever resulted from this killing. Entratta was brought back to New York, after having been captured in Chicago, and acquitted. Later he was found murdered. Diamond was away for a long time after the night at the Hotsy Totsy; he came in and gave up eighteen months after the killing, and was released in a few days. What had happened? No one was alive to give evidence against him. Weak little Hymie Cohen, business partner of Diamond in the Hotsy Totsy, who had ordered the orchestra to play loudly while the shooting was going on, was taken for a ride. Two waiters, who certainly could have told a story, were picked up dead.

But Diamond, though free, found New York uncomfortable. Neither the police nor the powerful racketeers wanted him around. He bought a little place at Acra, up in the Catskills, and played the part of a country gentleman: he sent his chauffeur to Albany to get medicine for a woman's sick child; he paid a carpenter to build a cowshed for a poor woman; he gave large tips at the country barber shop. And still no one loved him.

During these bucolic days in the Catskills Diamond's wife, Alice, was with him. Alice was a sketch. Among the furnishings of the house was a chair, wired for electricity, in which Mrs. Diamond took great delight. She invited her callers to sit in the chair. Then she would turn the switch and give them a shock. Diamond didn't like the idea, but Mrs. Diamond told him to get used to it, "because you may have to sit in one yourself some time."

Meanwhile Diamond tried to muscle in on some of the rackets in the Catskills, where applejack and bad needle beer were the favorite drinks. He had little success and came very near getting into trouble when Harry Western, a roadhouse proprietor, disappeared from the face of the earth. Diamond's chauffeur was found trying to dispose of Western's car by driving it off into the river in Brooklyn. But nothing serious came of this.

It was on Sunday, October 12, 1930, that Diamond had another brush with the guns of his enemies. He was in a room at the Hotel Monticello with his sweetheart, Marion Strasmick (Kiki Roberts of the Follies) when two men came in, kicked him around, shot him five times and disappeared. Amazingly, he recovered from his wounds.

No one wanted Diamond. New York didn't want him. The thumbs of the underworld were down. They feared him in the Catskills. When he went to Germany he was arrested and kicked out. Not even the English papers, who referred to him as "Cunning Jack," could make him feel at home.

On another Sunday, in April, 1931, he was at the
Arratoga Inn, near Cairo, New York, when he
stepped out on the porch near midnight. There was
a roar of pump guns, and Diamond crumpled up.
They thought he was dead this time, but he fooled
them again.

Diamond was indicted for kidnaping and torturing
James Duncan, a cider hauler. On the afternoon of
December 17, 1931, he was acquitted by a wool hat
jury in Troy which had deliberated only a few minutes. That night there was a celebration in an Albany speakeasy. At 1 A.M. Diamond told his wife he
had to go to a press conference to see some of his admiring friends from the newspapers. Instead, he
went to see Kiki Roberts, and then went to his own
room at 67 Dove Street. He may have been a little
drunk—must have been. There was a rattle of gunfire at 4:45 A.M. The landlady went up and found
him dead. One theory was that one man had held
him while another made sure that, this time, the bullets would finish him forever.

Mrs. Diamond, always the forgiving wife, who had
stuck to "Legs" since their wedding in 1917, and who
understood thoroughly that Jack's peculiar tempera-
ment made it necessary for him to run around with
showgirls, was the only mourner at the funeral.

Miss Roberts went away, quietly, to live her own
life. The house at Acra, with the electric chair, was

lost through foreclosure. Mrs. Diamond wound up
in Brooklyn. She drank a good deal, talked vaguely
of being "tired of protecting these mugs," and passed
much of her time in shooting galleries, where she made
high scores.

At 6 P.M. on June 30, 1931, Charles Hunter, superintendent of the house at 1641 Ocean Avenue, Brooklyn, opened the door of Mrs. Diamond's apartment
with a pass-key. She lay face down between the living room and the kitchenette. Her cheap print dress
was torn. She had been shot in the head with a .38
caliber revolver. She had been dead at least three
days. Her two pets, Belgian griffons named Speedy
and Whiskers, were terribly hungry, and lay whining
on the floor. It is entirely possible that she had talked
too much.

3. MARY LOUISE CECILIA GUINAN

Texas Guinan, in her fashion, during the boom
times of the twenties combined the curious and admirable traits of Queen Elizabeth, Machiavelli, Tex
Rickard, P. T. Barnum and Ma Pettingill. She was
known as the Queen of the Night Clubs. Her greeting "Hello, sucker!" became the watchword of boob-
traps from Wall Street to Hollywood. She was a
realist, hard, friendly and competent. Other women
might be superior to Texas as entertainers, but they

lacked her imagination and her executive ability. The year of the Repeal Vote found her in Chicago, where the seekers after culture went to view the Century of Progress Exposition.

During the long years of her New York enterprises she became one of the town's great figures. In one period she was supposed to have made $700,000 in ten months. She was most prosperous in that era when she was in partnership with Larry Fay. The thinkers of the amusement world discussed her gravely as an important social phenomenon, which she was. These important facts were recorded of her:

Once, by dieting and baths, she lost 40 pounds in a month; she goes to early mass on Sundays; she sleeps on her right side; she could round up 100 head of cattle when she was fourteen years old; she never takes a drink; she is a good poker player and lucky; her first husband was Julian Johnson and her second was David Townsend; she is good to her folks.

She came from Waco, Texas. Even before the war she was known in the theatrical profession, and for a time, in the films, she was called "the female Bill Hart." Soon after prohibition she became the best known person in New York's night life. She lived at 17 West Eighth Street, in Greenwich Village, a place full of gewgaws and folderols, where she relaxed and lived the quiet life during the day.

Texas, in her New York days, was primarily a host-

ess, certainly technically one, and this circumstance
always saved her from serious trouble when her clubs
got into trouble for violating the prohibition law.
She always insisted, blandly and with logic, that her
club didn't have to sell liquor to make money. She
said that most of her customers had flasks, and that
the profits came from cover charges, mineral water
and ginger ale. That was in the days when a club
could get as much for a quart of White Rock as a
quart of bourbon was worth before prohibition. Of
course liquor was sold—but Texas, cagy with the law,
let the head waiter attend to the booze selling on his
own responsibility.

By 1927 Texas had become a tradition. Her girls,
beautiful and sometimes talented creatures who went
onward and upward to big things, were called Guinan
Graduates. Texas was getting so much publicity that
even Aimee Semple McPherson came to town to try
to get a share of it.

When Emory R. Buckner was Federal District Attorney of New York and made his drive against night
clubs that sold liquor, one of his victims was the 300
Club, where Texas was appearing as hostess. There
were three counts: violation of a personal injunction
against the sale of liquor, possessing intoxicating
liquor, and the sale of intoxicating liquor. The first
was the most serious. She must go to jail. As they
led her away she had the orchestra play "The Prison-

er's Song," and at the station house she had no end of
fun twitting the raiders. The next month she was
cleared in Federal Court of the contempt and liquor
charges. Meanwhile she had received publicity worth
a fortune. She was brazen and irrepressible, always
the showman. They might padlock her clubs, but
she would always come free and flit to another spot.

In the summer of 1927 she opened "The Padlocks
of 1927." This revue was run like a night club. Her
whole gang was there, the little girls prancing around
with next to nothing on. Between acts Texas walked
around in the audience and bombarded Harry Richman with tennis balls. Backstage she would lay down
the law to the girls, like a harridan with a quirt.
When this show closed she opened a rowdy place in
the basement of the Century Theater, a sort of circus,
with a calliope, shooting gallery, fishpond and dart-
throwing board. It was a coin-trap if there ever was
one. There was more padlock trouble, more suits,
more injunctions and more publicity.

There were other clubs, other strange projects,
some of which were carried out. Others fizzled. In
1931 she decided to take some of her girls to France
to put on a show. Arriving there, she found that although the French didn't object to her performances
on moral grounds, they did object to her importation
of American performers and her scheme of taking
money from the French. It is dangerous to say

"Hello, sucker!" to a Frenchman. She came back to America, but by this time the depression, and a faint distaste of the authorities for the antics of La Guinan, convinced her that the racket was dead. She went away, on road tours, and finally wound up in Chicago.

Texas, to New York, was the star performer of the period when everyone liked to be spoofed. The secret of her success, probably, was her candor. She told people they were fools, and were being rooked, and they liked it. She was, at heart, a capable, pleasant and ingratiating individual, full of sound sense and a shrewd wit. Turned loose in a night club she could perform wonders. She might recognize an aged and wealthy dolt sitting alone at a table. She would try to convince him that he should play leapfrog. If he demurred (strangely enough, leapfrog frequently was just what the old coot had been wanting to play since the Boer War) she would rub his bald head, crack jokes at his expense, and the first thing anyone knew there would be one of the finest games of leapfrog ever seen.

Texas was sincere in standing up for the moral reputation of her girls. Some of them might have been no more strait-laced than they should have been, but when one of them began running around with a man whom Texas regarded as a bad one, she would give the girl a piece of her mind—and a piece of Texas's mind was pointed and vigorous.

She had what is known as a man's mind, which in her case meant that she reasoned as a shrewd male *entrepreneur* reasons. She could perform many acts of charity, and she was extremely generous, but she was not pulled and hauled by silly emotions. Most of the money she gathered in during the years of the great hoop-la was money which came from persons who were eager to spend it. Better take a sweetie to Guinan's club and have a whale of a night of it, than to invest it in worthless bonds or pay a big income tax. Texas, to be sure, was anti-social, but she and the suckers had a good time.

4. FAY AND THE SWASTIKA

It was the custom after the war to refer to Larry Fay as "the racketeer." He was at one time or another supposed to have been mixed up in rackets involving taxicabs, milk, booze and night clubs. He came out of Hell's Kitchen, and died by the bullet, but he never was convicted of any serious crime. He was by way of being a cheap brawler when he felt pretty sure that he was safe. His summonses and arrests totaled forty-six on the known record, mostly from lawsuits, quarrels, and bawling out policemen who had stopped him for traffic violations or other minor offenses.

Sometimes Fay had money and sometimes he didn't.

Most of his ventures were carried through on a shoe-
string. He would open a night club, without a cent
to pay for the help or the groceries and mineral water,
and stall off the skeptical by showing them his list
of reservations for the opening night.   In his last
days, when he was dreaming of starting a new night
club, he passed most of every afternoon in Moore's
restaurant, sitting with old Mr. Moore and little Jeff
Barnett, the sawed-off veteran of Broadway. There
he hoped for better times, and laid plans to get new
capital. In those last days, too, he was not above bor-
rowing a few dollars from a friend, and he was worried.

The truth appears to be that Fay had neither the
bold inclination nor the iron will to be an authentic
Big Shot among the racketeers. Time and again he
was on the verge of controlling profitable and fairly
legitimate enterprises, only to lose them to men of
harder temper—men who could be tough when they
said they were. Up to a certain point Fay could be
bluff and sure of himself, but he had no stomach for
a gamble with sudden death.

Fay was gaunt, tall, dark, heavy-faced, with the
suggestion of a horse about his profile. He wore a
large black felt hat, dark suit, black tie and white
shirt. He loved the night clubs, and he danced with
beautiful women. He looked sinister, but he was
anything but a killer.

As a boy he had been a bundle wrapper. He bought a cab and drove it for a while. All the West Side boys, and all the police, knew him. Once he went to the race-track and bet on a 100-to-1 shot, a horse named Scotch Verdict, and the horse came home in front. On the horse's saddle blanket was a swastika, and Fay adopted the swastika as his good luck emblem and put it on his fleet of cabs which he purchased with his new-found money.

For his cabs he hired very tough drivers—ex-convicts, old prizefighters with crumpled ears, and men from Hell's Kitchen who knew how to take care of themselves in a brawl. He did well for a time, and had some valuable hacking privileges, but he was worried by slit tires, and thuggery, and lawsuits. He sold out for a profit and opened a night club, which he called El Fey. Then came his partnership with Texas Guinan, the nights of "Fay's Follies," the big armored car, deals for large quantities of liquor, the acquaintance of men of wealth and importance, dress suits and bejeweled women. But he ran afoul of two things: the law from above and the muscle men from below. He had to close. He went to Florida, and failed there too.

In 1928 there was a great stir because it was suspected that the New York Milk Chain Association, of which Fay was practically the entire directorate, was a racket. Fay was investigated for many weeks, but

nothing ever came of it. Next he thought of his old
racket, the taxicabs, and tried to get back in that dangerous and heartbreaking business. He even had a
scheme under which he was to be the czar of all the
independent cab drivers in New York—the Judge
Landis or the Will Hays of the jehus.

Another fling at night clubs in 1932, this time at
the Casa Blanca, in the handsome building which once
housed the Club Napoleon in West Fifty-sixth Street.
It wasn't doing so well, but he had hopes of getting
by. He fell a victim, finally, to the Share-the-Work
movement which was popular in the winter of 1932.
On December 30 he posted a notice informing all
employees that their pay would be cut. Edward Maloney, a doorman, had been receiving $100 a week;
now he was to get much less, with shorter hours, and
another doorman would take his place during the
day.

On the evening of January 1 Maloney drew up to
the club in a cab and got out. He seemed to be
drunk, as he often was. He had his right hand in the
pocket of his blue overcoat. He asked Fay for his
pay. Fay sent an assistant upstairs to get it. There
were four shots. They found Fay near the entrance,
half on a sofa. He died very quickly.

Maloney was gone. He walked up to a traffic officer three days later at Sixth Avenue and Eighth Street
and gave himself up. He said that, following an old

custom, he had gone out New Year's and got drunk, and remembered nothing of what had happened. After a trial before Judge Collins in General Sessions, at which his lawyer, Dudley Field Malone, contended that the shooting must have been done by another man, Maloney was convicted. He was sentenced to Sing Sing to from eight to sixteen years.

Fay had a gift for the gaudy, the resplendent, and the high, costly foolishness of the night life. He deserved a more spectacular fate than to be killed by a drunk.

5. LITTLE BLACK MOSQUITO

Florence Mills was undeniably great. There have been other Negro performers who, depending on one's taste, may have excelled in singing, or dancing, or all-around artistry, but at her best this girl was the toast of the whites and blacks alike. She was the favorite of the crowds that began going to the hot spots of Harlem right after the war, after the discovery that Negro rhythm, Negro songs, even though they might be astoundingly vulgar, were high art because of their naturalness.

The crowds loved her at Les Ambassadeurs in Paris; at Baden-Baden, where she went when she wasn't feeling well; on Broadway, when she performed at the Palace; in Harlem, where she was queen, and on the steamship *Ile de France,* where the passengers es-

teemed her the most attractive of celebrities. Raquel
Meller was said to have been jealous of her. From all
the reams of adulation of her we find that "she looked
so like a droll, dainty creature . . . like a human-
sized mosquito who draws laughter instead of blood
. . . her skin not dark, but rich and burnished, and
more alive than whiteness . . . She has the genius
of the grotesque . . . Her body speaks." Hot-cha.
She had automobiles and all sorts of admirers. One
night Feodor Chaliapin, at the old Plantation, was so
moved by her performance that he tried to jump over
the ropes and salute her as a greater artist than he;
the great Russian was restrained by Percy Hammond
and Morris Gest.

Florence Mills was born in Washington in 1895 and
was brought to New York when she was three years
old. As a little gamin, she used to dance in the streets
of Harlem. When she was old enough she joined her
two sisters in an act called the Mills Trio. In 1916 she
joined Ralph Dunbar's act on the Keith Circuit and
there met U. S. Thompson and married him. Those
two other great Negro performers, Ethel Waters and
Ada Ward, were her friends and contemporaries. She
was always the artist, and the trick of her art lay
mostly in her sublime self-consciousness, which reminded some of the natural poise which Roland
Hayes has on the concert platform.

Beginning in 1923 her star rose rapidly. She

joined the cast of the Greenwich Village Follies, playing at the Winter Garden, and was a success. The
next year she appeared in "Dixie to Broadway," and
it was observed that she had unlimited range, being
able to sing anything from a ballad to a hot number.
Until she came, it had been difficult for a Negro
troupe to break through the theatrical Jim Crow line
and reach the inner circle of Broadway. Even Sissle
and Blake, and Miller and Lyles, had to work mostly
on the outskirts. But Florence Mills came straight to
the Broadhurst. In 1926 Charles B. Cochran took her
to London; there and in Paris she was acclaimed.

In the summer of 1927 her health began to fail.
The long tour with "Blackbirds" had weakened her.
She went abroad, visiting health resorts, but returned
to New York to undergo an operation for appendi-
citis. She delayed too long, and died on November
1, 1927. The obsequies outdid anything ever seen in
Harlem; certainly there was more excitement than at
any similar event since the death and burial of Lieutenant Jim Europe, the founder of the jazz band.
On the first day, as the little black woman lay in state,
13,000 persons, white and black and brown, filed past
her bier. On the third day the police said forty thousand in all had passed. When it came time for the
funeral there was a choir of 600, with music by 200
instruments. Inside the Harlem church and outside
along the dingy streets were 150,000. Hall Johnson

directed the choir. Jules Bledsoe sang. A cornetist
died of heat and emotion. The newspapers discussed
her passing in grave editorials, praising her contributions to amusement, and to the colored race. In London, where she had been particularly loved, the papers
printed encomiums of her grace and her peculiar
charm. She died almost as poor as a cotton field
Negro.

Florence brought them to Harlem, the crowds of
the night life age. People soon after the war began
to discover such places as Jimmie's, Small's, the Capitol and Palace Gardens, all Negro places filled with
laundry workers and elevator men. And there were
the aristocratic places, such as the Cotton Club and
the Exclusive Club, where the Harlem social leaders
preferred to go. With the great discovery that it was
smart to go to Harlem, thousands of spendthrift
whites deserted the resorts of Broadway and Greenwich Village and piled into Harlem. Soon most of
the crowds at the better places were one-third white.

There were all sorts and conditions of places: the
Hoofer's Club, composed largely of professional Ne-
gro entertainers who went there to be entertained;
the Club Cabaret, full of talent, and managed by
Johnny Cobb; the Nest and Small's, where they had
Monday morning breakfast parties that began at 5
A.M. and lasted until noon or later; the dozens of
small, rough places where, on occasion, there were

razor fights and it was dangerous for a white man to go.

Harlem, after the crash of 1929, kept up surprisingly well. Even in the summer of 1933 it was going strong. Legal beer injured the night life somewhat, but didn't kill it. Many Negroes, who formerly had drunk nothing but the traditional gin, began drinking the heavy, harmless 3.2% brew, a potion which has in it less fun but fewer fights.

Most of the brains back of the continued prosperity of Harlem amusement are in the skull of Lee Posner, a short Russian Jew who for many years has been an expert on the night spots of all New York. He was hired originally by Harlem night club proprietors to put the section on the map. He succeeded in making the Cotton Club and Connie's Inn as well known as the old Silver Slipper or the Salon Royal downtown used to be. Traditions grow up fast, and in Harlem they mushroom. It is largely due to the gossip and the information sent out by Posner that New Yorkers are familiar with Duke Ellington, who is known as the Paul Whiteman of his race; "Snake Hips" Earl Tucker at Connie's; Cab Calloway, the master "scat-singer"; Don Redman, author of "How'm I Doin'?", and dozens of other people and places. The place has come a long way from the war-time days, and the pre-war period, when Barron Wilkins, later murdered by a foolish Negro named Yellow Charleston, ran his old club, where, very rarely, white people would be allowed.

Some of it is filthy, and some of the joints are gyp places, but for people who like to stay out late at night it is like no other spot in America. There is no end of black talent. But they still remember Florence Mills, who was there in her greatness when the intelligentsia, along with the butter-and-egg men, first became Negro-conscious.

THE SHADOW OF THE VULTURE

THE old gangs, as such, already were virtually out of existence by the close of the war. A few remnants were left, spiritual descendants of the stalwarts of the Hudson Dusters, the Whyos and the Gophers, and they were busy with their relatively trivial enterprises—package stealing and fighting in the interminable wars of the labor unions. They were succeeded by "mobs," which were smaller groups, much more compact and efficient, who developed to a highly scientific degree such profitable enterprises as stealing payrolls and robbing banks.

Many of the more intelligent criminals, even after prohibition had been in effect several years, had no connection with the alcohol racket. Gerald Chapman, the fastidious and brainy mail robber who was hanged in Connecticut for murder, had no interest in liquor and its profits. The Whittemore mob, among whose members were the gifted Kraemer brothers, who found safe-cracking in the Stone Age and raised it to a fine modern art, preferred robbery to bootlegging. Not that they were above taking money from any illicit source, but their tastes and aptitudes ran to the more old-fashioned lines of banditry.

But for every one of these thugs who stuck to the

old ways, a dozen others went into one of the many remunerative branches of criminality or near-criminality which surrounded the making, the distribution and the selling of booze. The young sadist who had been beating up people for fun found that he could make real money as a strong arm man. The punk who couldn't hold a job as an honest truck driver turned out to be peculiarly gifted in transporting loads of booze in fast motor cars. The drugstore loafer, who had dreamed of possibly turning into a holdup man, could get work as a lookout for booze "drops" or speakeasies. And the proficient gunman, whose services as a killer had been in only infrequent demand, found that there was much serious and profitable work to be done.

And another subtle change began to be noticed. Business ethics steadily began to decline. Was there ever a period in which money was held in such high esteem? The old sacred things were not worth fighting for any more, but money was—and much of this money came, in any one of a hundred forms, from the industry which grew up to supply the nation's thirst.

One night in the summer of 1933, an ancient retired gunman, who is something of a philosopher in his homespun American fashion, leaned against the bar in a New York gin mill and observed:

"There will always be killings of passion, with a woman involved. What the French call the crime

passionel. But you don't hear of them so much any
more. People don't look at things like they used to.
Would one man kill another one today for stealing
his wife or sweetheart? Some would, but they would
be set down as hot-tempered. They'd either sue, or
forget about it. They don't get worked up over the
same old things. They kill now for money or for
power."

There is something in what the old man said. To
kill over a love affair indicates a certain lack of poise.
It is profitless and even naïve.

Moreover, there has been a change in the attitude
of the underworld itself toward that most damnable
of all crimes, kidnaping. To the general public, kidnaping is still the most cowardly and despicable crime
ever invented by the harpies of the human race. Once
the underworld itself, with curious unanimity, regarded the kidnaper as the lowest of creatures. That
isn't quite as true now.

It hasn't been long, as the years go, since the small
son of Col. and Mrs. Charles A. Lindbergh was kidnaped and murdered. There had been kidnapings before, to be sure, and the case of Charlie Ross was ancient history, but most kidnapings had been confined
to members of the criminal class. The Lindbergh case
was so hideous that it seemed almost unbelievable.

And yet, strange as it may seem to some, there was
a tremendous outcry against the Lindbergh kidnapers

from the underworld itself. On the day after the news of the crime became public, enraged gangsters, and even men who had served time for horrible murders and maimings, wanted to aid in the search for the guilty ones.

One notorious ex-convict, terrible in his fury, offered his services, and the services of his considerable organization, to Colonel Henry Breckenridge, lawyer for the Lindberghs. A few days later the Lindberghs actually accepted the services of Salvatore Spitale and Irving Bitz, two underworld characters, who were to aid as intermediaries. Hard-looking men, genuinely angry, reported at the offices of at least three criminal lawyers in New York, denounced the kidnapers and asked if there wasn't something they could do.

Most of these men had children of their own. Moreover, Lindbergh was a national hero. The affection of gangsters for their own offspring, and even for all children, birds and animals, although perhaps not always the touching and splendid sentiment which the romanticists would have us believe, nevertheless is often real enough. There also was, perhaps, another consideration: a crime like the Lindbergh kidnaping, which was sure to cause a violent flare-up against the entire underworld, would be bad for all the multifarious branches of the rackets—even the so-called legitimate rackets. In other words, it would give all the boys a bad name.

What happened? In the course of a few months the snatch racket, as kidnaping came to be known, had developed into a popular source of income for the underworld. It became a racket which, though sometimes risky, was more often than not successful. It is reasonable to suppose that not all the members of the underworld retained their first flush of noble resentment against kidnaping. It was still bad form, of course, to kidnap a child; that was the act of a rat, and no mistake. But how about a banker, a wealthy recluse, a man who could spare the money? Well, many of the snatchers felt that there was, after all, a difference. There had been a change in ethics. When one kidnaping mob is known to have at least nineteen members, it is reasonable to suppose that the underworld feeling against kidnaping is far from unanimous.

Loyalty was strong in the old gangs, but the modern mobs, particularly the mobs headed by such men as Al Capone, Bugs Moran and Dutch Schultz, demand loyalty of absolutely unquestionable quality. Treason, even when only suspected, is punished swiftly. In the booze racket, a tycoon, having amassed all the money he wanted, and hungering for the quiet joys of a farm or a home in Florida or California, would find that he could not desert the boys. To say, "I've had enough and I'm getting out," would be to sign his death warrant. The same principle

holds for the leaders of the kidnaping racket. The
end of the squealer, the deserter, or the man who pro-
fessed a desire to quit, would be as terrible as it would
be certain.

Members of the mobs are held in line with an effi-
ciency which would do credit to the Russian Cheka.
Men have been murdered merely because of a vague
suspicion that they were losing their nerve. The test,
said to have been invented in the Chicago of Capone's
greatest glory, is simple, and it is not particularly new.
It merely applies a psychological test which is as old
as the human race.

Suppose a killer begins to show the first faint signs
of weakness. Perhaps he doesn't eat as heartily as
usual. He requires a great deal of coffee. He drinks
booze when serious business is about to be transacted.
He sulks and broods, and looks furtively about. He
doesn't listen when someone asks him a question. Obviously something is wrong, but judgment must not
be passed too hastily. Perhaps the lad has had a hard
week. He may be able to pull himself together, but
meanwhile, it is decided to give him the laboratory
test to make sure.

One night the boys will take him on a tour of night
clubs or dance halls where there are plenty of girls.
At each place the girls will have been tipped off to pay
particular attention to the poor fellow who is suspected of losing his nerve. The girls will fawn upon

him, flatter him and even attempt to seduce him. If he responds, if his mood lightens, if he laughs with the girls and becomes enraptured over one or more of them, the diagnosis is that there is nothing seriously wrong. But if he passes the whole evening oblivious to the charms of the ladies, or sneering at their most assiduous attentions, or informs them rudely that he is not interested in their silly wiles, then he has brought in a verdict against himself. He is through and must be put out of the way. The end may come at some lonely roadside, or in a hotel room, or while he is walking along the street, but he is as good as dead. The principle of this test is summed up in the maxim: "Any mug that won't go for a dame is yellow."

It is probable that most of the killings among the more sinister elements have been done, not in anger, but to preserve discipline, to punish disloyalty or disobedience, to still a dangerously loose tongue, to remove a weakling, to convey a warning to rivals or to rub out a figure who might become too powerful in his own right.

Chicago gave to the language of the twenties and the early thirties the phrase, "He was taken for a ride." The system in general, however, is very old. It had its variants in the old West, where it was done by men on horseback on still, far-off ranges before the days of the fast automobile.

The student of social trends will find that up until

about 1926 when a man was taken for a ride he was almost always taken to inevitable death. It was strictly a no-return affair. There was much bewilderment in New York when, one morning, a disheveled wreck of a man was picked up in a thinly settled section of Staten Island. He said he had been picked up in Manhattan, placed in a car and carried out to the Staten Island woods, where he had been beaten and tortured and finally turned loose. But who had done it he would not say. His name was Charles Lucania, now known as "Lucky" Lucania, a power among the Sicilians. The men who kidnaped and tortured him ("Legs" Diamond, later shot and killed, was supposed to have led the group) didn't want to kill him. It was their way of conveying a message, but what this message was is a secret which not even the best detectives in the New York Police Department have been able to learn. The most plausible explanation is that the men wanted some money from another racketeer who was hard to reach.

The good old Sicilian custom of inviting the victim to a banquet, at which he would be lulled by food and wine and good fellowship before execution of the death sentence, had its charm, but viewed coldly, it was a time-waster and sometimes dangerous. The better practise, which evolved through many years of trial and error, is to put the victim into an automobile, bash him on the head, tape his mouth, and then, when a safe spot has been reached, shoot him and dump him out. Or, if ransom is desired and not murder, stop short of the shooting.

All the physical paraphernalia used in the snatch racket are for the most part refinements of the mechanics of taking people for a ride. The nice points of technique, mastered by the practitioners of the middle twenties, are useful not in kidnaping and holding for ransom. To be sure, some new brains, expert on conducting ticklish negotiations and writing notes and codes and passing money, have been called in.

Ride-taking in Chicago and environs was relatively simple because of the geographical layout. Chicago is a sprawling sort of place. Running out of the city are many roads, which make it easy to remove a victim expeditiously. In New York, which is a vertical city, the problem is not so simple. Skyscrapers, traffic congestion, and the difficulty in capturing a man in middle Manhattan and getting him safely out into the open country of Long Island or New Jersey, have placed a heavy strain on some of the most thoughtful criminals. Some stubborn men have saved their lives by remaining for weeks in their hotel rooms or apartments and refusing to budge. There isn't much that can be done with such a man until loneliness or lack of money drives him out.

No one, despite all the glib theorists of the underworld, ever has drawn up a sensible, workable code for taking a man for a ride. Some hold for one system, some for another, depending upon the habits of the victim, the ultimate purpose of the ride, and the physical difficulties involved. The most highly approved system, which works in many cases, is what might be termed the automatic ride-taking system, in which every man acts as his own grave-digger and, so to speak, puts himself on the spot.

An example: Suppose a man, as the quaint euphemism has it, "can't get well," which is to say, he "has the finger on him," which is a way of saying that he is marked for slaughter. He may suspect that there is a plot against him, or he may not. He is trailed until he enters a night club or a speakeasy. Inside it is arranged that he gets the best possible attention, particularly plenty to drink. It is best that he become pretty soundly squiffed. The mulish man, or the one who is cagy enough not to drink too much, sometimes must have something slipped into his drink. The point is that he should stagger out of the place, with his reasoning powers considerably befuddled. His first thought is to get a cab—any cab. One is waiting and he gets in. What he doesn't know until it is too late is that two or three men, in full possession of their faculties, are crouched in the back of the car. From that moment on he is entirely at their disposal. The poor chap has, to all intent, crucified himself.

Difficult? Well, sometimes it fails, but oftener it isn't even necessary to go to all that trouble. In the first few months of the New Deal men and women have been kidnaped openly—from their automobiles in an open street, from their sun porches, while sitting at dinner in their homes and while walking to work. The cases have been so many, and the victims so diverse, that it is no exaggeration to say that every man or woman who has money, or whose relatives have money, is a potential victim of the snatch racket.

Ordinary police work in many parts of the country, particularly in the larger cities, has been able to cut down the number of payroll and bank robberies, assault and robbery, gang killings arising from feuds, and all the traditional crimes of violence. But kidnaping is another matter. There is a feeling, growing stronger as public fury against the racket grows louder and more insistent, that something more than ordinary police work, sometimes more than ordinary laws and ordinary prosecutors, must be found before the ghastly thing can be stopped.

Who are the kidnapers? It will not cover the case to say that they were bootleggers who have been thrown out of work since 3.2% beer became legal. Some of the known kidnapers, it has been proved, formerly had been engaged in such occupations as bank robbery, forgery, white slavery and dope peddling, and had nothing to do with booze. Others have been identified as members of gangs which had a hand in all sorts of rackets—slot machines, gambling houses, vice and booze as well. It is a motley, tatterdemalion crew, and it is not sufficient to dismiss them all as cowardly rats whose only strength lies in a species of low cunning. Among the members of the kidnap crews are some men of much more than average intelligence, of more than ordinary physical courage.

They are hard to catch. The clues are usually few and of little use. The family often is afraid to call in the police, preferring to pay the ransom through secret intermediaries and go to any lengths to avoid any possible harm to the victim. In many cases the only clues (and it is astonishing how useful these have proved to be) were what the victim remembered from the physical details of the room in which he was held.

When young Charles Rosenthal, a Broadway playboy, was kidnaped in August, 1931, and released on payment of $50,000 ransom, he remembered very little that, at first, seemed of value to the police. But he did recall that late at night, while he was being held, he could hear music from two places, apparently night clubs. He also remembered a label on a bottle in the medicine chest in the bathroom. Edward P. Mulrooney, then Police Commissioner, and an old-fashioned detective who knows his New York, deduced from this the neighborhood, and he happened to be right. The gang was caught, convicted and sent up for long terms.

It was old-fashioned detective work, with the local authorities cooperating with the Federal men, that resulted in the capture of Harvey Bailey, escaped bank robber, in August, 1933, in a little farmhouse near Paradise, Texas. Bailey and his gang had kidnaped Charles F. Urschel, Oklahoma City oil man, who had been released on payment of ransom. Urschell remembered from the days of his captivity one significant thing—the time at which an airplane passed overhead each morning and afternoon. One Sunday morning he hadn't heard the plane. A check with the airplane lines located the probable area in which lay the house where Urschel had been held. And Bailey, smart, sinister and as desperate a man as the underworld ever spawned, was captured.

But what happened then? Two days later, in Illinois and Wisconsin, the police and Federal men, with airplanes, machine guns and a great organization for a man hunt, attempted to close in on a gang suspected of the kidnaping of William Hamm, a brewer, and others. The kidnapers made a clean get-away.

It is a terrifying, challenging racket. In the summer of 1933 President Franklin D. Roosevelt gave it his attention. He authorized Professor Raymond Moley, Assistant Secretary of State, a man who has a reputation of sorts in both economics and criminology, to make a survey of kidnaping. A Senate Committee headed by Senator Royal S. Copeland began holding hearings at which various opinions were divulged. Governor Lehman of New York urged a law making death the penalty for kidnaping and also advocating that the payment of ransom money should be made a felony.

Whatever may come of all this hullabaloo, and no matter how many foolish, hysterical or impractical suggestions may be given the force of law, the stark reality of the situation is more appalling than all the killings of gang warfare rolled together. The cost has been high and it apparently is getting higher all the time, although some authorities say that it is merely a "passing phase," a sort of fashion trend among the greedy members of the underworld.

In the known cases of kidnaping in the first seven months of 1933 the ransom paid would reach a total of at least $365,000. This figure does not take into account cases where ransom probably was paid but on which the police were unable to obtain a definite figure. To all this must be added the enormous cost to the taxpayer of the police investigations and the prosecutions. It takes great man power to track down a gang of kidnapers.

A survey made by Joseph A. Gerk, Chief of Police of St. Louis, showed that in 1931, in 500 cities, there were 279 cases of kidnaping; of this number, thirteen victims were killed, and sixty-nine kidnapers were caught and convicted. Mr. Gerk said he regarded his figures as an underestimate, as many cases were never reported to the police.

There seems little doubt that the kidnaping gangs are pretty well organized. Indeed, evidence has been found that indicates that some of the gangs now operating were busy with their schemes as far back as 1926. It started with gangsters kidnaping each other, and only rarely did the police hear much about it. Then it spread, with definite technique and plans of procedure, to the kidnaping of wealthy adults who were respectable members of society.

Alexander Jamie, chief investigator of Chicago's "Secret Six," estimated the number of kidnapings in 1931 and 1932 at 400, although only forty-nine were officially reported for the latter year. The Middle West, which always did produce desperate characters, appears to be far ahead of the rest of the country in bold and profitable kidnapings.

The incredible daring of the 1933 model kidnaper is illustrated by the case of the unfortunate John (Jake the Barber) Factor, the Chicago plunger and expert in weird finance. In the spring of 1933 his son, Jerome, a studious appearing lad, was kidnaped, and Factor paid $100,000 for his release. On July 1 old Jake the Barber himself was kidnaped by a dozen armed men, some of whom carried machine guns. He paid $50,000 for his release.

For a short time after his release there was considerable skepticism of the whole affair, for Mr. Factor's past would indicate that he was not above practising mild deception on his fellow men. But the investigators soon found facts which convinced them that there was nothing spurious about the snatching. Factor reported—and he apparently did everything he could to help the police—that his captors were obviously professionals, that they were highly organized, and that the band numbered at least nineteen men. They kept a list of their prospective victims. As a result of the Factor kidnaping the Federal authorities and the police began guarding some of Chicago's best known citizens, including Arthur Cutten, grain market operator; John D. Hertz, capitalist and former taxicab owner; Warren Wright, president of the Calumet Baking Powder Company, and Otto Lehmann, department store owner.

Would it help for the family of a victim to turn instantly to the police, tell all they knew, and keep the police fully informed of all negotiations? In theory, yes. Actually, few families have the courage to do this. Usually kidnaping is accompanied by a threat of death if the police are brought in—and there have been instances where this threat was carried out. The gangs are resourceful, and know what they are

doing. One victim was placed in a diving bell, low-
ered into water and almost suffocated before he would
agree to write the messages which his captors had demanded he write. In one den of kidnapers was found
a layout which undoubtedly was a torture chamber.
A man will agree to anything, sign anything, when
his feet are being burned, or when any one of the
many other modern refinements of the days of Tor-
quemada are being practised upon him.

There are some lurid tales of these organizations,
but none too lurid to be believed. There is, for example, the statement made by underworld experts
that back of most kidnapings is a sinister figure, the
brains of the plot, who is known as the Pedler. He
gives the gang the name of the man who can be kidnaped profitably and then he steps out of the picture.
Sometimes, so the grisly legend has it, he shops around
among several gangs until he finds the one who will
give him the best price for his information.

Next in the plot comes another brainy chap, known
in underworld language usually as the Finger. He
learns all he can about the intended victim, his personal habits, his bank accounts, his business deals, his
servants, the arrangement of his home, his peculiar
weaknesses if any, and everything else that may be
useful. The next important figure is the Spotter,
who must be a nervy, intelligent gunman. He leads
the gang on the actual snatching. Of course, masks,

handcuffs, bandages, bludgeons, guns and a satisfactory hideaway already have been arranged.

The most delicate part of the scheme, the negotiations for the return of the victim and the payment of the ransom, is left to another expert, a highly gifted man known as the Voice. This man gets a large share of whatever money is collected, for his is a ticklish rôle. If he made a mistake, he might face either sudden death or capture and sure conviction. He must arrange codes, use the telephone, devise fool-proof schemes for receiving the money. He must see to it that the bills are small, as large bills would be traced more easily; he must be wary of the chance that the victim's family has notified the police; he must keep his head.

What to do about it? There have been dozens of suggestions which might help, but meanwhile the racket grows worse. Will it increase? Many think so, among them Patrick Roche, Chicago's famous crime investigator. Many police officials hold that not only have many thugs formerly engaged in bootlegging turned to kidnaping as the profits from hard liquor became less, but that they are steadily recruiting an army of assorted criminals who would be bad news at any time, booze or no booze.

Police Chief Gerk of St. Louis had hopes that the Federal statute, passed in 1932, which may be invoked in cases where state lines have been crossed, would

help end the racket.   It didn't, although it made it
possible to use Federal men on kidnaping cases.

Lewis E. Lawes, Warden of Sing Sing Prison, tes-
tifying before Senator Copeland's racket hearing in
New York, said that the alliance between politics
and rackets must be ended—a perfectly commonplace
statement which evoked gasps from a few naïve lis-
teners who appeared to be hearing the news for the
first time that there was such an alliance.   The Warden said that if he had the powers of a Mussolini he
would invoke martial law, thereby ending all rackets
in short order.   Maybe, but his views appear somewhat academic.

More to the point was the testimony of George Z.
Medalie, the Federal prosecutor for the Southern District of New York, and Chief Justice Frederick Kernochan of the Court of Special Sessions, a Democrat,
who pointed specifically to the relations between the
gangs and the politicians.   They were not talking altogether about kidnaping but about the racket system without which kidnaping could not exist.   Said
Mr. Medalie:

"Gangs are part of the machine for municipal control and not until politics is divorced from municipal
affairs will we get rid of the gangsters."

He offered to name at least four New York political leaders who were in league with the gangsters, but

Mr. Copeland apparently regarded that as outside the committee's scope.

Said Justice Kernochan, who once served as an Assistant District Attorney in the homicide bureau when the great William Travers Jerome was District Attorney of New York County:

"Gangs exist because they have some usefulness connected with district leaders. In between elections, the gangsters guarded gambling houses and did other strong-arm work, but their special work was performed on primary days and election days and that is how they got protection from district leaders. They couldn't exist a minute—no, I won't make it that strong, but they would be given a tremendous blow if somehow the protection of district leaders could be taken from them."

Even the police, said Justice Kernochan, are far from free from the influence of the gangster-politician alliance. "God help a policeman that the politicians are down on!" exclaimed Kernochan. "He might as well leave the force or pound the pavement. He hasn't a chance." Then he said:

"I suppose it is lese majesty to say the police force is not 100 per cent efficient. It is composed largely of wonderful men but some of the men, not the Commissioner, perhaps, but some of the high officials, are very susceptible to the approach of men with political influence."

For some reason the statements of Mr. Medalie and Justice Kernochan were regarded as rather astonishing, though what they had to say is a matter of common knowledge to anyone who has had even a passing acquaintance with the workings of political patronage, political wirepulling, wardheeling and skullduggery in New York City—or, for that matter, almost any other city of any size.

Out of all this comes the idea that a way might be found, somehow, to remove the police from the influence of politicians. It is possible, not to have the millennium, but to have something approximating a clean police force. Such a force, with its handcuffs removed and the shadow of influential gangster-politicians lifted, could clean up any community reasonably well in short order. And it wouldn't need martial law.

Would a strong Federal police force, paid for out of Federal funds, operating as a strong, well-knit unit, cooperating with local officials wherever needed, solve the problem? Some experts, among them former Commissioner Mulrooney, believe that such a system might be of assistance, though it has drawbacks. This "American Scotland Yard" idea is not new; it is revived every now and then when the local police seem to be helpless against any particular crime menace.

The objection is this: A strong Federal force, even if large and well equipped, might be under political

influences just as dangerous, just as deadening, as local
police are at the present time in many cities. Moreover, during the long years of prohibition, the Federal officer became the symbol of oppression, identified somehow with the snooping dry agent, and
there was a vast decline in the prestige of everybody
connected with the Department of Justice. Some of
these operatives were regarded as not very bright;
others were suspected of being downright crooked.
And where would the master detectives come from
who would make up the personnel of this great Federal force? Who would appoint them? Would they
really be trained, competent men, or would they owe
their places to a slipshod scheme of patronage? There
are the problems; from their solution may come the
answer to whether the Federal Government can or will
be successful in its move against all rackets, including
kidnaping.

Here is one phase of criminality where the frequent
complaints against the American jury system do not
apply, for there never has been any difficulty in con-
victing the captured kidnaper. Stricter laws and
harsher penalties? In some states the penalty for kidnaping is death, but there are two schools of thought
as to the effectiveness of this. One holds that the
death penalty will be a powerful deterrent; another
contends that it is dangerous, that it will cause the

kidnaper to murder his victim to remove the chance of capture.

Another suggestion is that the whipping post would be the most chilling of all deterrents to the kidnaper. Mr. Mulrooney, ordinarily a kindly man, in advocating the last points out that he has listened to many stories of torture, and he believes that the kidnaper should be treated as harshly as the kidnaper treats his victim and the victim's family. He does not believe his suggestion will be adopted, the humane school of modern penology being what it is, but he does know that the criminal fears the lash more than he fears prison, gunfire or even the chair. Another defender of the whip for the kidnaper argues that the old objection to lashing, that it had a brutalizing effect upon the man who wields the cruel weapon, might be removed by inventing a mechanical gadget, a sort of electric cat-o'-nine-tails, which would do the work upon the mere pressing of a button.

There are, of course, innumerable other ideas which are put forth as aids to curbing all types of crime. Universal finger-printing and a Federal law for the regulation of firearms have many supporters. Both of these reforms—if they are reforms—appear to stand a better chance of adoption now than ever before. The objections to universal finger-printing rest upon nothing more than a vague feeling that somehow it interferes with the privacy of the citizen, that

it makes everybody suspect. The objection to strict
Federal regulation of firearms goes further back into
the history of the American people and their traditional belief that there is something sacred in the
right to bear arms.

Americans, from pioneer days on, have been notoriously fond of firearms. More than any other people on earth, they are gun-crazy—or, as they said of
the late Frank McErlane, the Chicago gangster who
was always shooting, "gat-goofy." When murder is
to be done, the weapon is the revolver, the shotgun or
the machine gun. Is there any reason why machine
guns should be sold to gangsters? And yet in one
year seventy-seven machine guns were sold by one
firm in New York City. In the bloody months that
followed, these weapons began turning up all over the
country—after massacres, bank robberies, kidnapings
and other underworld high jinks. Surely there is no
excuse for the machine gun except in the military or
police forces.

Given all these things—a cleaner police force, a
Federal detective organization composed of superior
men, universal finger-printing soon after the cradle,
the regulation of guns—what then? The racket owes
its existence to the lethargy or the cupidity or the
fear of the ordinary citizen, especially the business
man who, by trying to outwit his competitor, has recourse to the services of gunmen, acid-throwers, fix-

ers and strong-arm experts. Then there is the banker who takes the accounts of known gamblers and worse. He must stand his share of the blame.

It is Caspar Milquetoast, home-lover, bridge-player, and fine fellow, who has put himself on the spot. Caspar has let himself be put upon. He has tolerated corrupt political machines, or turned them out for machines that were just as corrupt. In any case he has not protected himself, and usually he hasn't even tried. There are many instances of where a business man had sand enough to stand up and tell racketeers to go to hell; sometimes he has come to a horrible end, but in many others he has emerged a hero.

It is a lot to ask the families of a kidnaped man to tell the Pedler, the Spotter, the Voice and their band of cutthroats and torturers to go to hell. Perhaps it is asking too much. And no one could reasonably expect Caspar to turn, overnight, into a Spartan and a raging lion compact in one little human breast. And yet, if he only would, there would be an end to all this horror—this shadowy, spidery thing which, in the memory of persons of middle age today, once was almost unheard of, but which now hovers over every home in America from which utterly conscienceless bands may expect to squeeze blood money.

THE VILLAGE AND BARNEY GALLANT

GREENWICH VILLAGE, they always say, is not what it used to be; the old place, where there was love and musty comfort and high hopes, is dead, passé, and all the people worth knowing have moved away. But this complaint contains only surface truth; underneath it is as false as the smile of a Greek clip joint proprietor. For each generation, according to its own romantic or intellectual inclinations, creates a Village somewhat in its own image. And when members of that generation come back, years later, after wandering in quest of phantoms in the Bronx, or Brooklyn, or some other far-off lonely place, they complain that the place has changed.

To be sure it changes, but not greatly through the years. John Reed is gone, and he had not been dead in Russia three years before his contemporaries, embittered by the passing of the old days, were saying that the Village was no more. To some, the period immediately following the war was splendid, and the Village of that remote time takes on a misty glamour. Youngsters say in 1933 that you should have seen the Village in the marvelous boom years of 1928 and 1929.

Vast real estate developments in the late twenties changed the face of much of the sprawling section below Fourteenth Street.   Into some of the new apartment houses came people who had no spiritual kinship with the free souls who had been striving for remote dreams in attics and dirty basements.   Al Smith moved from Oliver Street to lower Fifth Avenue.   J. Irving Walsh, responsible for much of the building of the new apartments, killed himself in his home in one of his tall buildings overlooking Washington Square, where the children play.   Howard Scott, who years ago used to propound his abstruse theories of Technocracy in Romany Marie's, much to the delight of Marie, saw himself touted as a new prophet and then forgotten.   Raymond Orteig couldn't hold out for prohibition to be repealed; he had to give up the Hotel Brevoort, and in 1933 people, rather self-consciously, began patronizing the new sidewalk restaurant in front of the old hotel. Don Dickerman, who ran the Pirate's Den, the Blue Horse and other goofy resorts, went bankrupt.   People came and went, but the Village, in its essence (which, if it means anything, means that people felt comfortable living there) remained about the same.

No more genius in the Village?   No more genuine talents budding there?   Ridiculous!   It is probable that in 1933, when many of the new-fangled apartments are vacant, there are just as many young men and women living there, hanging on to existence by their toe-nails, who will amount to something as there ever were. The region, of course, always has had its share of freaks, nuts and fakers; indeed, some of the same ones have been there for at least twenty years. But the others, the youngsters who are trying to get started and who live there only a few years at most, are the ones who will become the writers, painters, dramatists and dancers. They come in droves. Most of them drown themselves in gin, Chianti and free loves; they become bums, move away or settle down to nothing. But there is always the residue which amounts to something. If they have no money, they eat in the little tea rooms or the lunch places on Sixth Avenue. Or they go farther down, to Bleecker and West Houston and Prince streets. If they are in funds, they can go to Barney's, or the Lafayette, or Mori's. The worst thing that happened to the Village during the prohibition years was the failure of the supply of decent wine. It may be that cheap gin, fresh from the bathtub, and drunk in one's own apartment, can prove a powerful stimulus to creative work, but the weight of authority is on the side of good cheap wine, drunk on rough wooden tables in some low restaurant where the food is sound but inexpensive.

The great man of the Village, today as for many years, is Barney Gallant. He is the most important philosopher of the region, and one of the most expert purveyors of entertainment on earth. He probably knows as many people as Jack Dempsey, Edward P. Mulrooney, James J. Walker or James A. Farley (all expert rememberers with wide acquaintances).

Moreover, Barney occupies an important spot in history. He was the first man in New York to be sent to prison for violating the prohibition law. It seems a long time ago, but the memory is fresh. In 1919 George Baker, owner of the Greenwich Village Inn, died, and the resort was purchased by Barney, Frank Conroy, Hal Meltzer and Mrs. Margaret Barker.

The Prohibition Act, which prohibited the sale of beer, wine and distilled liquors until the conclusion of the war and termination of demobilization, went into effect at midnight on June 30, 1919. It provided maximum penalties of one year in a jail, a fine of $1,000, or both. Since the law lacked teeth, the Volstead Act was passed over President Wilson's veto on October 28, 1919, and genuine prohibition went into effect on January 16, 1920.

Barney's place, the Greenwich Village Inn, was perhaps the most popular place in the Village. All sorts of people came there, including the members of the Greenwich Village "Follies," which was playing nearby. Gallant was a pleasant fellow. He kept on selling booze to everybody who was thirsty and who had fifty cents. He was raided in October, 1919, and

arrested for selling liquor. Similar charges were made
against six of his waiters, and the charges against them
were considered stronger than those against Gallant,
since he had not actually been caught making a sale.

Barney was brought to trial before Judge Learned
Hand in the United States Court, Southern District
of New York. He offered to plead guilty and take
whatever punishment might be coming if the charges
against the waiters were dismissed. The court agreed.
Judge Hand sentenced Barney to thirty days. Years
later Barney said the real reason he took the plea instead of letting the waiters take a chance was that the
head waiter was on the verge of becoming a father,
and had a bad case of pre-natal jitters.

The doors of the Tombs, that smelly old prison into
which leads the Bridge of Sighs from the Criminal
Courts Building, opened for Barney. They housed
the Federal prisoners in the Tombs in those days, before the Federal Government built its wonderful new
detention pen. Immediately Barney became the most
popular prisoner in America. He bought cigarettes
and chocolate bars for all the other inmates; he gave
liberal tips to the guards, who liked him, and everybody had a good time. His friends, however, were
upset. They worried Judge Hand and the prosecutor, Joseph Mulqueen, Jr., Assistant United States Attorney, so much that Barney was brought back into
court after only four days in the Tombs. Said Mul-

queen, addressing the Judge in the presence of the immaculate Barney:

"May it please the Court, since this man was convicted I have not had a moment's peace or pleasure. I have been besieged with pleas to let this man go. Even a police captain and a priest have come to me. But I am unalterably opposed to leniency in this case."

Judge Hand, who all through the prohibition era was one of the handful of Federal Judges who appeared to remember that all the rights of man had not been superseded by the dry law, gave Barney a ten-day reprieve to set his business affairs in order. After that Barney served sixteen more days. While he was out on reprieve he learned that his friends were circulating a petition for his release. He urged them to stop, which they did after getting more than 20,000 signatures.

Barney, in December of 1921, opened the Club Gallant at 40 Washington Square South. It was easily the swankiest place in the Village—no place for a starving artist to pass the evening, but perfect for those who had money. During the early part of the twenties there was an amazing influx to the Village. These people were of all sorts: youngsters with strange stirrings in their breasts, who had come from remote villages on the prairie; women of social position and money who wanted to do things—all sorts of things—

in a bohemian setting; business men who had made quick money and who wanted to breathe the faintly naughty atmosphere in safety, and ordinary people who got thirsty now and then and wanted to sit down and have a drink.

The previous generation had given to the world a great many well-known writers and artists who had lived for a time in the Village. These people gave the place great publicity, all of which stressed the happy-go-lucky aspects of life below Fourteenth Street. Some of this ballyhoo, of course, was sheer nonsense, but it brought the people. The general attitude of the section toward prohibition also had something to do with its popularity during the first years of the dry law. The Village, true to its reputation as a hell-hole, probably was the easiest place in New York to get a drink.

So they came to the Village, and Barney, with his new Club Gallant, was the first to put the tall silk hat and the coat tails upon raffish bohemia. His prices were as high as those in the best night clubs in the Park Avenue and Broadway areas. The place was as exclusive as any in town. Indeed, there were nights when it was almost as hard to get into the Club Gallant as it is to get out of the prison at Dannemora. Only the cream of wealth and society could get in—except, as always, Barney's old friends, who came and paid if they could.

Barney's idea at this time was that the big places uptown were mistaken in having big shows, with many girls and hoop-la. He wanted to get away from the floor show idea. He built a stage, with boxes for the patrons, and he himself was master of ceremonies. His program consisted of sketches, good vaudeville skits, and he depended strongly upon an atmosphere of intimacy.

The Club Gallant in those days charged $16 for a bottle of Scotch and $25 for champagne. If a man had a bill of less than $25 he was never quite welcome again. The club occupied the lower floor of the building, and was decorated with panels which bore the likeness of noted people in society and the theater. Never did Barney permit any drunkenness or rowdiness. A soft and tolerant man in his quiet moods, he can be so hard that it isn't safe to leave him alone with himself.

In 1924 Barney closed the Club Gallant and opened a new place to the south, at 85 West Third Street, where he carried on the old Gallant tradition for six more years. His place had its ups and downs, but always it retained a high class clientele. Barney is a man who can change his philosophy with the times. For example, in 1925 he drew up a list of rules for the night club life. The depression, years later, made them all unnecessary, but at the time of their promulgation they were sound:

1. Reserve a table in advance so as to be sure of admittance.

2. Do not offer any gratuities to the head waiter or the captain as soon as you enter the door. If the service was satisfactory tip one of them a moderate sum upon leaving.

3. Bring along your own "atmosphere" with you. It avoids controversy and is much safer all around.

4. Do not get too friendly with the waiter. His name is neither Charlie nor George. Remember the old adage about familiarity breeding contempt.

5. Pinching the cigarette girl's cheek or asking her to dance with you is decidedly out of order. She is there for the sole purpose of dispensing cigars and cigarettes with a smile that will bring profits to the concessionaire.

6. Do not ask to play the drums. The drum heads are not as tough as many another head. Besides, it has a tendency to disturb the rhythm.

7. Make no requests of the leader of the orchestra for the songs of the vintage of 1890. Crooning "Sweet Adeline" was all right for your granddad, but times, alas, have changed.

8. Do not be overgenerous in tipping your waiter. Why be a chump? Fifteen per cent of your bill is quite sufficient.

9. Examine your bill when the waiter presents it.

Remember even they are human beings and are liable
to err—intentionally or otherwise.

10. Please do not offer to escort the cloakroom girl
home. Her husband, who is an ex-prizefighter, is
there for that purpose.

Following is Barney's sermon on the ideals and the
moot points of the night club racket:

"Exclusiveness is the night club's great and only
stock in trade. Take this away and the glamour and
romance and mystery are gone. The night club manager realizes that he must pander to the hidden and
unconscious snobbery of the great majorities. It is
because they make it so difficult of access that everybody is fighting to get into them. . . . My headwaiter was offered on one occasion $50 by a man who
seemed rather intelligent if he would seat him next to
Nita Naldi. The offer was refused. Neither pleas
nor all the bribery will get you the coveted ringside
table from the headwaiter unless he thinks, in his
own estimation, that you deserve it. . . . The offer
of a tip by a patron as soon as he enters the doorway,
with hope of obtaining a good table or better service,
immediately stamps him as a yokel. His display of
gold does not achieve him anything but contempt. . . . Big society people seldom give big tips.
They feel they are doing the place a favor merely
by being there."

It was in January, 1932, that Barney shocked a

great many fine old families by moving to 19 Washington Square North. The North Side of the square always had been barred to commerce and amusement. Wanamakers and Rhinelanders lived there. The Washington Square Association, an organization formed to keep the square and the neighboring streets as chaste as possible, kicked up a fuss when they learned that Barney was going to open the very exclusive Washington Square Club in the old Shattuck mansion. He answered that he was doing the square a good turn by giving it a high class restaurant and center of entertainment which would draw celebrities from all other parts of the city. There was still some grumbling, but Barney opened the club. It was a success in spite of the depression.

The place is dripping with historic associations. It is four stories high, with a high stoop. It was the scene of one of the most startling crimes ever committed in New York. On April 2, 1922, Albert R. Shattuck, a retired banker, was forced with his wife and servants into their wine cellar by four French thieves, one of whom, a desperate character named Gabriel Alphonse Mourey, once had been a butler in the house.

The wine vault was so tightly closed that Shattuck feared his wife would suffocate. He worked on the hinges with a pocket knife and a ten-cent piece. In thirty minutes he succeeded in opening the door. He

ran up the stairs to give the alarm and found the
thieves still in the living room, apparently dividing
the $80,000 in jewelry which they had taken. The
gang broke up and ran. One of them was caught
outside the house, but the others went away.

Shattuck now had an interest in life. He wanted
to track down those missing three thieves who had
robbed him and so nearly killed his wife. He took
personal charge of the man hunt. It took him two
years and $50,000 to do it, but all of the robbers were
finally arrested, convicted and sent to prison for long
terms. He was sixty-nine at the time of the robbery.
He died on November 5, 1925—the hero of all good
citizens.

In 1932 the people who weren't playing bridge
were playing backgammon. Barney, in the old Shattuck house, capitalized on these fads by outfitting the
second floor of the house into game rooms. Nobody
uses these rooms much any more, as people in 1933
stopped playing so many games, partly because of the
general cheapening of entertainment, such as cheaper
shows.

Barney's last place is exclusive enough, and it still
draws all sorts of charming people, but it is far from
being the high-toned establishment that the old Club
Gallant set itself up to be. Styles have changed. The
celebrated Arnold inspects guests with great care.
No one who is not known can enter. The place is

roomy, there is a floor for dancing, a five piece or-chestra, a circular bar, and excellent French food. The club can take care of 120 persons at a time. What will be the fate of such places when prohibition is repealed is a matter which no one, not even the sagacious Barney, can foretell. It is probable that his place, and a few others like it, will continue to oper-ate, as exclusive clubs, very much upon the present plan. They have, for one thing, a clientele which remains fairly steady.

The man Gallant, who often scolds himself with the epithets "Liar!" and "Thief!", was born in Riga, the Latvian city where so much erroneous news comes from, on May 1, 1884. His parents were Jewish, and Barney says his great-grandfather went into Rus-sia with Napoleon's Army. Napoleon scurried back through the snow, but grandpa stayed in Russia. This old fellow, who was so small that he could walk under a table without stooping (some say while wear-ing a top hat), and who lived to be 104 years old, founded a large brewery in Riga.

Since that time all the Gallants, who are scattered through America and Europe, have been at least com-fortably well off, and some of them have been wealthy.

Barney Gallant (the name is spelled Galant in the French and Russian editions of the family) studied under tutors until he came to this country in 1903

and landed at Baltimore.   Although he could not
speak a word of English, he was no fool, and had little
difficulty in getting to St. Louis, where he had two
wealthy uncles.   One of them, Uncle Henry Gallant,
was one of the most gifted pawnbrokers in the Western World.   He sold watches by the barrel or the keg
and was a man of parts.

Barney learned to speak English in three months.
Then he learned to write English, living meanwhile
off the pawnbroking uncle.   With this groundwork,
he started as a cub reporter on the St. Louis *Star,* and
later went to the *Post-Dispatch.*   He studied all the
time, sometimes toying with the idea of becoming
an engineer.   In 1909 he went to Chicago for a brief
stay and then moved on to New York.

In New York he met Eugene O'Neill.   In 1910 and
1911 Gallant, O'Neill and Louis Holliday, now dead,
lived in a one-room apartment in West Fourth Street.
The room was cold, had no electric lights and next to
no furniture.

The next few years were precarious.   Barney did
some free-lancing for the newspapers and was able
to get along.   In 1914 a delegation of Mexican school
teachers came to New York, and Barney wrote some
stories about them which attracted the favorable attention of the Mexican junta, which had headquarters
at 120 Broadway.   Although he spoke no Spanish
then, he was hired as Carranza's press agent.   He

made three trips to Mexico City, lived in the palace for a time, and taught the Mexican leaders all he could of modern American publicity methods.

When the United States entered the war Barney made a deal with the secret service, agreeing to quit the Mexican government if the agents would stop shadowing him. He came back to the old Village, where everyone knew him, and where he liked everything—the artists, the writers, the chiselers and fakers, the staid old families, the charming old houses, the dives and the quiet little restaurants.

He knew all the great ones, and those that were almost great—O'Neill, Theodore Dreiser, Edna St. Vincent Millay, Susan Glaspell, Zoe Akins, Will Irwin, Inez Haynes Irwin, John Sloan, George Luks, the Barrymores and that endless succession of people who at one time or another had something to do with the section. He knew Noel Coward in 1922, when Coward lived hungrily in Macdougal street. Coward submitted skits for the Club Gallant, but Barney never used them.

For years he has sworn that he would not leave the Village. Because he knows the club business, he has received many excellent offers to move uptown among the whales and the sharks of the racket, but he prefers to stick to the place he likes.

Barney is of medium height. His hair is black, turning gray, and it sticks up above an oval face with black eyes, giving him something of that look of mild but perpetual astonishment which reminds one faintly of the expression of George Jean Nathan. He dresses with great care. He speaks rapidly and sharply. He doesn't smoke, but he will drink anything in reason. He takes no exercise and has no use for athletic games. He won't even watch them. He has never married, but he addresses half the women who come into his place as "Mrs. Gallant" and they seem to be flattered by it.

Like most of the people who find their living or their pleasure in the night life of New York, he never goes to bed before 5:30 A.M. He lives in an attractive apartment on the first floor of the old house at 45 Washington Square South. He arises at noon, visits his club and checks up on his staff of high-priced hired help, and then goes back to his apartment to talk with friends. A Negro maid keeps the place in order and mixes cocktails when guests drop in during the afternoon.

Barney, almost every summer, travels extensively abroad. Wherever he goes he finds people who know him and who are glad to see him. He is proud of being a Jew. He is rabidly pro-British and prefers traveling in England to all other countries. He is an exceptionally shrewd business man, though he has his radical side. In culture and intelligence he is as far above the ordinary uptown night club proprietor

as Santayana is above Dopey Benny Fein. Most of the
others have exhausted their resources when they say
it may rain tomorrow, or that President Roosevelt
seems to be a good man. Not so with Barney, who
can, and usually does, talk for hours on everything
from Marxism to the modern novel. He belongs to
no movements. "No isms or cults are any good,"
he says. "Every man should be his own Jesus."

His Village has been declining as a playground since
the great depression, but it is still lively enough, still
the pleasantest, most easy-going section of New York.
The streets are not quite as dirty as they used to be;
the horrible old women's prison has given way to a
rather good-looking new jail; the tall apartment
houses have altered the skyline a bit. But the place
is essentially the same. Says Barney:

"Remember the kids. They will always be here.
Some of them will bloom and from them will come
the next crop of well-known folks. The talent is always here."

Most foolish of all civic movements have been the
occasional outbursts of various organizations in the
section who have sought to make the Village as nearly
as possible like any other part of town. Most of these
campaigns have been fostered by real estate interests
who wanted to bring to the Village a class of people
who pay higher rents—and to hell with art and long
hair. All these movements have failed, as they de-

served to fail.   The Village must always be pre-eminently the home of cheap gin, of red ink, of little family bars, and of tiny, rather dingy apartments where young people hatch their lofty plots to outwit a sordid world.

THOUGHTS OF AN OLD FUDDY-DUDDY
WHILE SITTING

(Or, *Anybody Can Do This Sort of Thing*)

GEORGE BELLOWS, just before his death, patiently expounding his defense of an alleged indecent picture: "Art strives for form and hopes for beauty." . . . Jed Harris, sitting at a prizefight and undergoing more intense agony than either man in the ring. . . . Dr. John Roach Straton, of the sepulchral voice, pointing to the rude chairs which he had made for his bride years before and declaiming, "You know, the Master was a carpenter." . . . Owney Madden, turning to Walter Winchell and snarling, "You louse! You think you know so much about Broadway and you never heard of Doody Broderick!" . . . Charles Francis Potter, the Humanist, and his admiring tales of the great deeds of Oom the Omnipotent. . . . William J. Guard, looking more like Robert Louis Stevenson than Stevenson looked, lying in his coffin. . . . Frederic MacMonnies, the sculptor of "Civic Virtue" in City Hall Park, defending his private opinion that it was the best of his works. . . . My first meeting with Edwin C. Hill, the great reporter, who mistook me for an office boy. . . . A last train ride with James J. Corbett, obviously dying but able to growl in his rich barytone, "I'll be all right, boys." . . . Whit Burnett and the amazing brown beard which he brought back from Majorca.

Texas Guinan, one afternoon in the old Stork Club, whispering to a friend, "I hear they snatched Big Frenchy last night." . . . J. Frank Dobie, the "Pancho" of the brush country in the Southwest, patiently enduring a literary tea. . . . Walter Davenport the night in Jimmy Kelly's, when he believed the Apache dance was real and chivalrously rose to the defense of the girl. . . . The old San Quentin graduate who gave me the friendly smile as I picked him out of a line-up at the Tombs for misdeeds that sent him on a long stretch to Sing Sing. . . . Keats Speed, most understanding of managing editors, walking seventy feet to say a kind word to a reporter. . . . Frederic F. Van de Water, tall and white-haired, and his formal greeting, "Good evening, Commissioner." . . . Joel Sayre, former bodyguard to Admiral Kolchak, giving the supreme rendition of "Frankie and Johnny." . . . Captain Stephen Norton Bobo, leaping from his automobile to paint a landscape that had attracted him. . . . Herbert Hoover, as Secretary of Commerce, reading in a dull monotone a speech he had written for a small gathering at the old Waldorf. . . . Senator Huey Long,

king of the canebrakes, sitting up in bed in the New
Yorker Hotel eating peanuts.

Don Skene's definition of an old cow-country
word: "A maverick is a lamister dogey." . . .
Dashiell Hammett's old assignment when he worked
for the Pinkertons—to find a Ferris wheel which had
been stolen in Sacramento, California. . . . Cameron
Rogers, in top hat, morning coat and striped trousers,
touring the countryside on New Year's Day in a
rented Rolls-Royce. . . . A memory of Richard A.
Knight, now the most amusing of New York lawyers:
a little boy with a large head riding a bicycle down
Guadalupe Street, Austin, Texas, and reciting Byron
aloud. . . . Henry L. Mencken, barging down Fifth
Avenue during the dull days of the Coolidge administration and wishing for another war. . . . Ruth
Hale, wife of Heywood Broun and most articulate of
the Lucy Stoners, denouncing me in Barney Gallant's
for some ancient injustice. . . . John Nance Garner,
Vice-President of the United States, and his friend,
Edward Angly, newspaper man and author of "Oh,
Yeah!", taking a drink, which they called "striking
a blow for Liberty." . . . James W. Elliott, of the
old Business Builders, sitting at a table at the Algonquin and expounding the technique of selling
cemeteries. . . . James J. Montague's stories of his
long service with the quixotic William Randolph
Hearst. . . . Alice Roosevelt Longworth giving her

dinner-table parody of her cousin, Mrs. Franklin D. Roosevelt, speaking over the radio, a great bit of mimicry.

The deadly, close-clipped command of Captain Patrick McVeigh of New York Police Headquarters as he turned to his strong-arm squad during a raid on a "clip": "Toss this joint in the street." . . . The gentle Adolph, who cultivated tobacco plants on the roof-top speakeasy, now closed, where Dudley Field Malone once had had his pent house. . . . The proud terror of Herbert Asbury the week he thought he had been threatened by gangsters. . . . The pathetic incredulity of Geoffrey Parsons when he was told that, in many parts of the country, cemeteries are the most popular spots of assignation. . . . Ring W. Lardner, coming in drenched after the Dempsey-Tunney fight at Philadelphia and announcing that Tunney would be "the most popular champion since Tommy Burns." . . . Gene Buck, sentimental old song writer, propounding his belief that when love is weighed against duty and all else, "one woman's hair is stronger than the Atlantic cable." . . . Gene Fowler joining me one Sunday afternoon in hiring an open hansom cab to convey us to a meeting of hoboes on the East Side, where James Eads How presided. . . . William Muldoon, the Solid Man, sitting in his "hygienic institute" in Westchester and showing his sentimental side—his deep affection for Kid

McCoy, the bad boy of pugilism. . . . Owen Oliver, who, when past sixty, smoked twelve cigars a day and walked from his office at 280 Broadway to his home in Yonkers. . . . Robert Livingstone, New York's first bluestocking reporter, and his memories of Paddy the Pig, once-famous dive keeper.

Martin W. Littleton, lawyer, eating at the Lunch Club of Wall Street and pointing to another lawyer with the remark that "there goes an astridulent zither." . . . Owen P. White, the grizzled plainsman, and his tales of the feuds and tangled politics of New Mexico. . . . Hector Fuller, who was Jimmy Walker's writer of scrolls for distinguished guests during the years of the Great Madness, and his embarrassment when he erroneously referred to Queen Marie of Roumania as "Your Imperial Highness." . . . John Francis Curry, close-mouthed leader of Tammany Hall, in the days when he was a district leader and a writer of eloquent and bitter letters. . . . William J. Fallon, criminal lawyer, putting on one of the greatest shows of his life conducting the defense in the Bronx of a little chauffeur named Fritz, on trial for killing his sweetheart, and getting an acquittal. . . . Louis Bromfield, in the days when he worked for the Associated Press and toured the newspaper offices late at night checking up on dull items. . . . Frank Sullivan, fresh from Saratoga Springs, in the precarious days when he and

I were cubs under William A. Willis on the old *Herald*
at Herald Square. . . . Silliman Evans, Fourth Assistant Postmaster General under the New Deal, and
the time he was almost fired from a paper for spell-
ing "sergeant" correctly because his boss thought
it was spelled "sargent." . . . The astonishingly
pointed nose of Felix, major-domo at Madame Mori's
place in Bleecker Street. . . . Griffo, once the most
scientific of fighters, sitting in his later days, bloated
and coarse, catching live flies with his lightning-like
paws and releasing them unhurt for the amusement
of street gamins.

William O. McGeehan, the old Sheriff, explaining
to a young man who had been drinking too much
that one particular specter, a sinister fellow with hip
boots, dinner jacket and fireman's helmet, was a
harmless fellow once you got to know him. . . . The
curious belief of many persons that Edward P. Mulrooney, former Police Commissioner and now in control of New York State's beer, is a heavy drinker,
while the truth is that he never drank, not even
3.2% beer. . . . Harry Staton, former circus press
agent, singing hymns from 5 o'clock in the afternoon
until 3 o'clock in the morning and getting them all
perfect. . . . Bob Clifford, managing genius of society funerals, arguing that William Jennings Bryan
should not be buried in Arlington Cemetery. . . .
Leo Newman, the ticket broker, who, when meeting

a new acquaintance, likely as not will pull out a new necktie and give it to him. . . . Georges Carpentier and the beautiful women who lolled about him on the porch of his training camp at Manhasset the day after he was beaten by Dempsey in 1921. . . . Julius Tannen, the monologist, coming back to New York in 1933 with an iron-gray toupee making him almost unrecognizable. . . . Abner Rubien, the great mouth-piece, telling about what a whale of a wrestler he was at Cornell. . . . Nunnally Johnson, deeply moved at the funeral of Zip, the circus freak.

Percy Hammond, quivering with fright the day after he had been gypped in a fly-by-night speakeasy, and his relief when the place was broken up. . . . Chester T. Crowell, who can eat three heaping plates of tripe in an Italian restaurant, and who, though highly literate, pronounces it "len'th" and "stren'th." . . . E. E. Paramore, author of the immortal "Ballad of Yukon Jake," sitting in a corner at the Brevoort. . . . Beverly Smith, the old quarter-miler of Johns Hopkins, who, though the most cynical of men, writes success stories for a magazine. . . . Armstead R. Holcombe, the good gray editor, at whose behest I once had the prostitutes chased off Riverside Drive. . . . William Archer Sholto Douglas, author of "The End of Oofty-Goofty," who made himself an expert on the dialect

and folkways of many parts of America. . . . Clare
Briggs, in the days before his last illness, when he
wore a yellow coat, wing collar and stick, hat cocked
on one side and was the life of the party. . . . Richard Reagan, who covers the New York waterfront,
and his practically interminable recollection of the
time when he almost became a Trappist monk. . . .
Enrico Caruso, the day he was able to leave the
Vanderbilt after his long illness. . . . Reginald A.
Wilson, the Canadian, handsomest of all reporters,
who dropped dead on the station platform in Albany.

Charles B. Falls, proud of his lithograph of the old
Everleigh Club in Chicago as it looks today. . . .
John F. Hylan, former Mayor, and his splendid denunciations of what he called "art artists." . . .
Herbert Bayard Swope in a poker game with Gerhard
M. Dahl, a battle to the death between the two greatest extraverts of the Western World. . . . James
Stephens, the Irish writer, drinking Irish whisky in
the home of the late Cornelius J. Sullivan, New York
lawyer. . . . Nicholas Murray Butler, and his anger
when it was called to his attention following a speech
at the Metropolitan Opera House that he had said
"neutrality don't." . . . Julian Starkweather Mason
and his elegant long cigarette holders. . . . Lucius
Beebe and his Tattersall waistcoats. . . . The touching grief of Thyra Samter Winslow at the death of
her pet dog, Lobo, a superannuated Pomeranian. . . .

The explanation of Joab H. Banton, former District Attorney of New York County, that the initial "H." didn't stand for anything but was there merely because he liked it. . . . Col. Oscar H. Fogg refusing to acknowledge the greetings of a man he didn't like at a dinner at the Astor, and remarking to no one in particular, "I like clean things."

James W. Barrett's lengthy song which he developed from a limerick based upon the doings of the late Chile Mapocha Acuna, stool pigeon of the vice squad. . . . Silas Bent and his patronizing greeting of "Young man." . . . Julian Street Jr. being bawled out by his father-in-law, Frank A. Vanderlip, for being late at a lunch at the Union League Club. . . . Laurence Stallings, before the days of "What Price Glory," expounding his theories of literature over a table at the Newspaper Club. . . . Eddie Jackson, the photographer, and his almost reverential love for the memory of Woodrow Wilson. . . . The jokes cracked by the late Harry Reichenbach, press agent, when District Attorney Edward Swann summoned him in connection with a fake drowning in the Central Park lake. . . . Detective Edward T. V. Fitzgerald of Headquarters, who, when pressed, will exhibit a bullet imbedded just below the skin in the calf of his leg. . . . Bruce Gould, sitting at the Rhinelander annulment trial in 1925, barely able to control his amusement at the fantastic evidence. . . . Frank

W. Wozencraft, once the boy Mayor of Dallas, Texas,
learning the ropes of New York, from the University
Club bar to Madison Square Garden. . . . Earl Car-
roll, pale-faced, long-haired and smiling wanly,
lunching at the Lambs.

Joe Cook and his fabulous place at Lake Hopat-
cong, New Jersey, where, in the living room, are sus-
pended every imaginable object that is no larger than
a man's hand. . . . Dexter Fellows, the great circus
press agent, who, when told that the show was stu-
pendous and dazzling, waved his hand deprecatingly
and said, "I wouldn't go that far." . . . An afternoon in a New York apartment listening to the greatest tale of adventure of the twenties, the story of
J. Frank Norfleet, the Texas rancher who lost his life's
savings to a gang of confidence men and who trailed
them to the ends of the earth and caught them
all. . . . Al Smith, on his way to a Democratic pic-
nic in Chicago in 1925, sitting up most of the night
on the train singing old songs. . . . Walter Howey,
drinking brandy in a drawing room on a Pennsylvania
Railroad train and telling of the old days in Chicago
newspaperdom, the days of "The Front Page." . . .
The yachting parties of Larry Schwab and the fast
set of the North Shore of Long Island. . . . Steve
Hannegan's tale of his wild, lonely drive through the
Middle West to find his favorite surgeon and have his
appendix removed. . . . Kent Watson, who, in the

early days of prohibition in New York, accompanied
the agents on most of their liquor raids. . . . Phil
Stong, who once hung around the Criminal Courts
Building but who later made money and had Young
Otto come to his apartment to give him boxing les-
sons. . . . Freddie Wildman, now planning to import wine from France in large quantities, engaged
in long conversation with John Perrona, proprietor
of the old Bath Club in West Fifty-third street.

Father Wilfrid Parsons, one of the most articulate,
engaging and realistic of priests. . . . Whitney Bol-
ton, the most Broadway-struck young man who ever
came from South Carolina. . . . Larry Smits, the
bald lion of the tea parties. . . . B. O. McAnney
and his realistic imitations of tree frogs, best performed late at night. . . . Stuart P. Sherman, who
came to New York a shy professor from the Middle
West and had begun to like the place before he was
drowned. . . . Gene Tunney, delivering a lecture to
a panhandler who had poked his head into Tunney's
cab, and then giving the bum a quarter. . . . The
late Harriette Underhill, motion picture critic, who
came back to Broadway from Saranac to work and
die. . . . The Rev. J. H. Randolph Ray of the Little
Church Around the Corner and the ex-convict forger
whom he sought to befriend, to no purpose. . . .
Harold Ross and his almost pathological fear of cross-
ing bridges in a cab. . . . Dan Williams, the crusad-

ing editor, and his gestures as he inveighs against evil.

Lulu Vollmer, when she lived in Eighth Street before she wrote the play, "Sun-Up." . . . The exciting wedding of Morris Gilbert in the old church in Hudson Street. . . . George Gray Barnard, hair waving, discoursing in organ tones in an apartment in West Seventy-second Street. . . . Holger Lundberg, the Swedish poet, who can say "Thank you" in more different ways than any man in New York. . . . Justice Peter Schmuck of the New York Supreme Court, explaining that he drew upon Carlyle for his amazing prose style, which is the marvel of the New York bar. . . . James Thurber, very tired, sitting quietly fondling a French poodle. . . . Ross Santee, the artist, as gentle a soul as ever came out of the desert. . . . Cornelius Vanderbilt, Jr., who, as a cub reporter on the old *Herald*, used to come to work in his automobile, a strange sight in those days. . . . Oliver H. P. Garrett, who is now wealthy in Hollywood, and his consuming fear the night before he left New York that he would not make good. . . . The spectacle of David Belasco and Benny Leonard in earnest conversation at a prizefight.

The Hahn girls from Chicago—Helen, Emily and Josephine—and how they captured New York. . . . Ishbel Ross, who suffers dreadfully from seasickness but who passes most of her spare time on the ocean. . . . Dorothy Parker, the night she set out

deliberately to razz a Grand Duchess. . . . Selma
Robinson, the ablest go-getter among the women
press agents. . . . Fannie Hurst, looking pretty
bored at a crime prevention lunch at the Cosmopoli-
tan Club. . . . Edith Haggard, who is good enough
to laugh at even the feeblest jest. . . . Neysa Mc-
Mein, thrilled at the propect of being allowed to ride
an elephant in a circus parade. . . . Amelia Earhart,
the most attractive and the most sensible talker of all
the woman flyers. . . . The Poillon Sisters, from
whom Heaven deliver us.

Otto Liveright, and his incessant worry about his
health and the state of his psyche. . . . Bert and
Edouard, who have kept the resort known as the
Basques on a high level despite the depression. . . .
Elvin N. Edwards, the Long Island prosecutor, and
his after-dinner story of the capture of Arthur Barry
and Boston Billy Monahan, the jewel thieves. . . .
Jimmy Hayes, the little busybody, who never had
a steady job but who has seen almost every historic event, beginning with the Sullivan-Corbett
fight. . . . W. Axel (Baron) Warn, with his tales
of high adventure in Central America. . . . Bain-
bridge Colby, whose urbanity never fails. . . . Frank
A. Munsey and the night he took Albert J. Beveridge
to the Dempsey-Firpo fight and got there too late for
the excitement. . . . Courtenay (Brick) Terrett,
now alleged to own three polo ponies on the West

Coast. . . . Al Powers, the dreamy soldier of fortune who came out of Mexico and who now has an office on Park Avenue. . . . The bulk of Thomas Wolfe.

My senseless but continual surprise that there is a lawyer named Hyacinthe Ringrose, a prizefighter named Popper Stopper, a press agent named Fice Mork, a splendid chap named Damon duBlois Wack and a woman in Harlem named Floy Perfect. . . . The somewhat unholy and unreasoning amusement caused one night when it was learned that the Rev. Christian Fichthorne Reisner had injured himself while belly-busting with some small boys down a hill near his church in the snow. . . . The many arrests of Tommy Guinan, brother of the sainted Texas, in prohibition raids, and his perpetual immunity to conviction. . . . Andrew Freeman, on his return from Siam, and his account of the strange doings in Bangkok. . . . Arthur S. Draper and his steady pounding for idealism, the high spirit of youth and the amateur spirit, and the night he was guest of honor at a big dinner at the Vanderbilt at which a valuable statue was broken. . . . Charles S. Washburn, press agent who used to be a trick bicycle rider under the name of The Great Fearlesso. . . . Arthur Kober, now a scenario writer, sitting in a Long Island house one hot night with his shirt collar open. . . . Francis Albertanti, wise and cynical expert on the inside of professional sports, and his identification of a popular character, "Just a con man, but a nice guy." . . . The night in the Park Avenue Club where I saw Bill Corum for the first time since 1920. . . . The night in 1920 when Tris Speaker, then manager of the Cleveland Indians, came into Moore's restaurant with his ballplayers and all shucked off their coats because it was so hot.

The curious truth, probably of little importance, that there are two Tony Weirs; one Tony Weir, a big fellow, used to be a bartender at the Knickerbocker, while the other, a short man, has looked out for the public welfare both before and during prohibition. . . . Tim Shine, old saloonkeeper and the yarns of how he kept every cent he ever made. . . . Paul Mellon, son of Andrew W. Mellon, sitting in a café and planning to go to work for a bank. . . . Tony Muto, who got the "bends" by going down with the sand-hogs under the Hudson to write a story about it. . . . John Stewart Bryan, the tall, gray, Virginia publisher, and the night he was charged with being head of the Confederate Army. . . . William Macbeth and Wilbert Robinson, rotund and Rabelaisian, and great friends. . . . Sam Untermyer, Mephisto, flower-lover, great lawyer, riding through the Bronx in his Mercedes late at night and quoting Tennyson's "Locksley Hall." . . . Lawrence Tibbett, fresh from one of his early triumphs at the Metro-

politan Opera House, dropping in at a near-by
oasis. . . . Larry Fay at 4 o'clock in the morning sitting with a beautiful woman in Reuben's. . . .
Joseph Shalleck, criminal lawyer, reeling into a political headquarters in the old Hotel Marlboro one night,
bleeding from a beating suffered at the polls.

Franklin D. Roosevelt, tall, lean, dark, amazingly
alert and eloquent, captivating a group of women in
an uptown club with a speech just before he
was stricken with infantile paralysis. . . . Marquis
(Gimpy) Curtis, one of the smartest of criminals,
being captured by Detectives under Inspector John
D. Coughlin in an apartment on the West Side. . . .
Dr. Francis Carter Wood, the cancer specialist, and
his lifetime work of exposing fake cancer cures. . . .
David Hirshfield, later a Magistrate, trying to joke
with a waitress at the lunch counter of the Hotel
Pennsylvania. . . . Mike Haggerty's terse description of a garment worn by one of the women involved
in the murder of Joseph Bowne Elwell. . . . Artie
Hitchman, the little ticket hawker, the freshest kid
on Broadway. . . . John McHugh Stuart, the mys-
terious journalist who brought about the conference
which resulted in the forming of the Irish Free
State. . . . Richard Maney's first remark on recover-
ing consciousness after having been knocked out by a
Jew whom he had been chaffing in a barroom: "Cus-
ter in the Ghetto." . . . Donald Henderson Clarke,

his new Packard, and the great change that came over the old playboy of Park Row. . . . William E. Haskell, Jr., laying down the law to a policeman.

J. J. Conklin, the Chinatown tipster and derelict, whose constitution has survived Bowery smoke and Bellevue Hospital's ministrations. . . . Tex Rickard and the fine cigars he used to pass out; they were supposed to have cost him $1 each. . . . The dark and unsuccessful scheme to steal the silver leg of Peter Stuyvesant from the vault under the church of St. Mark's-in-the-Bouwerie. . . . Eddie Roberts, the Eastern impresario of greyhound racing, and his frantic search for a satisfactory press agent. . . . A. Barr Gray, who died on a beach in New Jersey, and who knew more policemen and detectives than any other person in New York. . . . Tom Gallagher, ancient billiard player, whose favorite food was applesauce and who never wore an overcoat. . . . William B. Hanna, the sourest of men, who once criticized a Florida landscape on a perfect morning because there were too many palm trees for his taste. . . . Christie Bohnsack, Tammany's smooth, competent arranger of receptions, parades and dinners. . . . A last telephone conversation with Frank Ward O'Malley the day before he sailed for France, where he died. . . . Martin G. McCue, former pugilist, a Tammany power who was so square, and so generous that he died without money, but he had a grand funeral at St. Patrick's Cathedral.

Fiorello H. LaGuardia, the little flower of reform, and his querulous voice over the telephone. . . . Paul Henkel, who used to manage Keen's Chop House, and the morning he helped me pacify a raging, knife-throwing, coat-room attendant who had been slugged for insulting a guest at a supper. . . . Tony Murphy, the linotype operator who plays the races and is by way of being a Broadway Big Shot. . . . George Auer, smacking his lips over the new beer at Luchow's and repeating, "My! My!" . . . Old Man Buckley, the quaint character who had made his shirt front into an electric advertising sign. . . . An evening with Caspar Hodgson in his amazing gun room under his garage on his Yonkers estate, an eerie place. . . . Dr. Leo Michel, Broadway's physician, talking of how his heart had been broken, or very near it, and believing it. . . . Captain William H. Wells, West Point's able public relations expert, and his unutterable disgust at being transferred to a far-off army post. . . . An evening with Joe Gordon, trying to convince him that he should run a paper in Ireland, all to no purpose. . . . John E. Rosser, earnestly wagging his right index finger and lecturing on what he calls the tempo of Broadway.

Myron C. Taylor, chairman of the board of United States Steel, wearing dinner clothes and watching the returns come in on the night of the Roosevelt land-slide. . . . Jack Johnson, the big smoke, giving an afternoon sermon on clean living in a Harlem Negro church. . . . William Travers Jerome, in his last fling in support of reform in the municipal election of 1921, smoking innumerable cigarettes and snarling his scorn of loose public officials. . . . Inspector John J. Sullivan, in charge of New York detectives, presiding at the line-up of criminals at Headquarters and tearing into each prisoner with a savagery that suggested that he must have done something to Sullivan personally. . . . An unfortunate brawl at Reuben's old place on Broadway, which ended with two beautiful women carrying out a battered and unconscious actor head first. . . . Morris Tremaine, Comptroller of the State of New York, having a glass of legal beer with the boys and discoursing upon the excellent quality of a forthcoming bond issue. . . . Detective Hugh Sheridan, gray-haired, probably the most suave and gentlemanly of all of New York's thug-hunters. . . . Harry Benge Crozier telling everybody that he had just rediscovered O. Henry and found him great. . . . The amazing energy of Grantland Rice, probably due to clean living. . . . Louis Fehr, heftiest of New York journalists, who can, and does, toss off a Scotch highball in one gulp, which is no mean trick.

The unimportant but rather curious fact that I

have never met, or seen, or talked over the telephone
with O. O. McIntyre. . . . The unbelievable face
and the scrambled vocabulary of Philly Lewis (born
Luigi Filippi) as he attempted, in Duffy's Tavern, to
conceal the fact that he couldn't read. . . . The
handsome mustaches of Stanley Sackett, manager of
the Madison, who looks and acts like an improvement
on the visions of Peter Arno. . . . Ned McIntosh,
the misanthrope, and his insistence that he must live
in a pent-house. . . . Eddie McBride, the veteran
artist, and his high-pitched, complaining voice. . . .
Dr. John C. Moorhead, great surgeon, and his tales
of the broken bones of men from war time on. . . .
John D. Rockefeller, Jr., walking with his boys down
Fifth Avenue on an Easter morning. . . . Alva
Johnston, best of all reporters, doing more work over
the telephone in an hour than a dozen leg men could
do in a month. . . . Burton Rascoe, stammering in
his excitement, recalling the rough old days in Chicago. . . . Ward Greene, and his willingness to forget that he had been reported dead and his obituary
printed in full.

Jimmy Walker on a Staten Island ferryboat giving
advice to a consumptive who was about to go away:
"Don't stand up if you can sit down; don't sit down
if you can lie down." . . . The Rev. Dr. Charles H.
Parkhurst, at eighty-five, sitting in a hotel room just
off Broadway and chuckling about how he could hold

his liquor on his underworld tours back in the nineties. . . . Joseph Canavan, devout Irish Catholic, and his whole-souled devotion to Governor Herbert H. Lehman of New York, a Jew. . . . Peter Molyneaux, sun-baked philosopher from the plains, who comes to New York once a year and discusses economics and current trends with the best minds. . . . John C. Kelly, the advertising man, publicist and political adviser, and the night he was upset because there was no liquor on the steamship *Rex*. . . . Samuel Hoffenstein, minnesinger, in the boom times when he helped make Al Woods a national figure. . . . James (Dinty) Moore packing up some hams and chickens to send to an unfortunate in Sing Sing because of that old West Side loyalty. . . . E. B. White, who married the charming and competent Katherine S. Angell. . . . Clarence DuBose, and his shudders at the memory of the Japanese earthquake. . . . Tom Steep, the Connecticut mandarin, longing for China.

Col. Charles A. Lindbergh, sitting with four at dinner and admitting that he hadn't any idea what the strategy in the air would be in the next war. . . . Don Marquis, most patient of men, laying aside his work in the evening to listen to the pointless conversation of two uninvited bores. . . . Langdon McCormick, the old scenic designer, and the afternoon that he thought he had discovered that Ibsen and I were alike in many ways. . . . William S. Chase, the music

critic, the Boy Scout who never grew up. . . . Carl
Hood, once a Tennessee financier, who came to New
York after the crash and raised tropical fish in Greenwich Village. . . . F. Porter Caruthers, and his ob-
session with crossword puzzles to the exclusion of
wars, earthquakes and sudden death. . . . F. Darius
Benham, promoter of iridescent dreams, and the
strange wax effect on his mustache. . . . Allan
Reagan, gambling for drinks with matches in the
Artists and Writers Club. . . . Harry Puck, song
and dance man, drinking Scotch under his apple tree
in Great Neck. . . . Ik Shuman, and the deep and
abiding affection that Paul Block has for him.

Lord Northcliffe, a few months before his death,
sitting in his suite at the Gotham and observing that
there were two great news situations—prohibition
and the fact that there were so many more women
than men in England. . . . Ward Morehouse, the
night he brought two chorus girls to a stag
party. . . . Philip Wittenberg, labor lawyer, and his
contempt for practically everything. . . . The consistent excellence of Nelson Hyde, husband of Thyra
Samter Winslow, in all games of skill, from bagatelle
to ping pong. . . . Edmund Duffy, the Baltimore
cartoonist, who has mastered the art of repose. . . .
The Fu-Manchu beard of Forrest Davis, principal
witness at the hanging of Gerald Chapman and the
elevation of Bishop William T. Manning. . . . The

abiding cynicism of Joseph Mulvaney, Hearst's great rewrite man. . . . Mildred Paxton, the week before she went back to Texas to become the bride of Dan Moody, who later became Governor. . . . Earl Reeves, perfect householder, who can cook, do interior decorating and chop trees. . . . The infinite poses and the essential soundness of Franklin Pierce Adams.

Will James, the cowboy artist, puzzled and sick on his first trip to New York. . . . John Bleeck, club owner, and his diatribes against crooked prohibition agents. . . . Robert Barton Peck, who, though busy in New York for more than twenty years, still has his chief interest in the early Indian troubles in Western Pennsylvania. . . . The blush of Joseph Phillips, who, excepting Irvin S. Cobb, is the only man ever to come from Paducah, Kentucky. . . . Heywood Broun trying to disguise himself so he could pass the night in the Municipal Lodging House without being recognized, a palpably impossible feat. . . . John W. Goff, New York's last Recorder, at the reception for Eamonn de Valera in 1920. . . . The dinner table banter of Alexander Woollcott. . . . An evening with Frank E. Campbell, the undertaker, at Janssen's old place, and his straight-faced, blood-chilling jocosity. . . . The girl who used to smuggle notes out of prison for her sweetheart, in the belief that, somehow, he might get out in less than ten years. . . .

Jack Sharkey, in his hotel room, yelling to a waiter to throw a raw steak through the transom instead of bringing in an ordinary dinner.

A murderous appetite, and a breakfast of bacon and eggs near the water at Fire Island. . . . A little island in Lake George, amid the clear water, where there are neither bucket shops nor clip joints nor traffic jams. . . . A roof on Central Park South, very late at night, with no noise except distant music and the low hum of far-off motor cars. . . . A walk along the Palisades at dawn, and the sight of New York's skyline unfolding and the city coming to life. . . . The unforgettable sound of a human head hitting a concrete floor. . . . Time for one more before we catch the train.

INDEX

323